WITHDRAWAL

Creating Tomorrow

WITHDRAWAL

Also available from Network Continuum

Leading Change in Schools – Sian Case

Schools and Communities – John West-Burnham, Maggie Farrar and George Otero

Understanding Systems Leadership – Pat Collarbone and John West-Burnham

The Constant Leader – Max Coates

Spiritual and Moral Development in Schools – John West Burnham and Vanessa Huws Jones

Regenerating Schools – Malcolm Groves

Creating Tomorrow

Planning, developing and sustaining change in education and other public services

Pat Collarbone

network
continuum

Continuum International Publishing Group
Network Continuum
The Tower Building   80 Maiden Lane,
11 York Road   Suite 704, New York
London, SE1 7NX   NY 10038

www.networkcontinuum.co.uk
www.continuumbooks.com

© Pat Collarbone 2009

British Library Cataloguing-in-Publication Data
A catalogue record for this book is available from the British Library.

ISBN: 1855394766 (paperback)

Library of Congress Cataloging-in-Publication Data
A catalog record for this book is available from the Library of Congress.

Typeset by Newgen Imaging Systems Pvt Ltd, Chennai, India
Printed and bound in Great Britain by Cromwell Press, Wiltshire

This book is dedicated to all those in schools
and other public services who are engaged in
changes that will improve outcomes
for children and young people.

Contents

Foreword by Michael Barber   ix
The Author   x
Preface   xi
Acknowledgements   xiv

1 The imperative for change   1

2 Remodelling: the early days   13

3 Remodelling: extending the agenda   27

4 Remodelling: the process   43

5 Remodelling: making it work   59

6 Remodelling: the change team   69

7 Remodelling: the critical importance of leadership   91

8 Sustaining change   105

   References   109
   Index   113

Foreword

The challenge of education reform has two aspects to it: getting the policy right and securing successful implementation. The first is difficult and the subject of a stream of publications, variable in quality but endless in quantity. The second is even more difficult but, oddly, barely touched on in academic literature. Maybe this is because those who have not been at the sharp end of delivering reform find it hard to understand the challenge of delivery, let alone write about it. Or maybe it's simply that 'what?' is an easier question than 'how?'.

In this outstanding book, Pat Collarbone brings her deep understanding of the sharp end of delivery to a fascinating account of how to implement reform. Between the Scylla of command and control and the Charybdis of laissez-faire, Pat and her colleagues created the National Remodelling Team to implement the workforce agreement that government and the unions had signed. They developed an active, collaborative style that engaged both national leaders and those at the frontline. They refused to take 'no' for an answer but reached 'yes' through a combination of demonstration, argument and persistence.

I enjoyed my interactions with them as they pursued their approach; I enjoyed seeing their evident success; and now I've enjoyed reading this excellent account of what they did.

Education reformers will need a variety of different approaches to implementation if the promise of reform is to be realized. We desperately need to build the evidence base to answer the question 'how?'. This book is a significant contribution to the emerging literature. Puzzled reformers the world over – there are many of them – will find it full of insight. Sometimes they will rightly choose command and control; other times they will devolve and seek to unleash success. Other times again, if they find people of the calibre of Pat Collarbone, they will choose her middle way. All of them will enjoy her book.

Sir Michael Barber

Sir Michael Barber is the founding head of the Prime Minister's Delivery Unit in the UK and is the author of *Instruction to Deliver: Fighting to Reform Britain's Public Services* (Methuen, 2008).

The Author

Professor Dame Pat Collarbone DBE, EdD, MBA, BA (Hons), FRSA is an education consultant and advises a number of public bodies including the National College for School Leadership (NCSL), the Training and Development Agency for Schools (TDA), Learning Skills Council (LSC), Lifelong Learning UK (LLUK), Department for Innovation, Universities and Skills (DIUS) and Department for Children, Schools and Families (DCSF). She is an acknowledged expert on school leadership and remodelling.

Pat was formerly a Director of NCSL and the Executive Director of the National Remodelling Team (NRT). She was a leading figure in the successful integration of the Teacher Training Agency (TTA) and the NRT to form the TDA. In September 2006 she formed Education Change Associates Ltd, an education consultancy firm, while continuing to hold a key role as Executive Director of the TDA. She is a Visiting Professor at Canterbury Christchurch University.

For 28 years Pat taught in inner London. She was a very successful headteacher of a secondary school in Hackney. In 1996 she founded the London Leadership Centre at the Institute of Education. Pat received a DBE in 1997 as an acknowledgement for her services to education. This is her most recent book. Her previous book, *Systems Leadership*, was co-written with Professor John West-Burnham.

Preface

This book describes and explains remodelling, the powerful and proven change process that has been the driving force behind the most exciting story in education in years – what Ofsted calls in its 2007 report, *Reforming and Developing the School Workforce*, 'a revolutionary shift in workforce culture' (page 6).

This culture shift has come about as a direct result of the successful implementation, through remodelling, of the 2003 agreement, *Raising Standards and Tackling Workload: a national agreement* (Social Partnership, 2003), between the government, employers' representatives, the school workforce unions and professional associations.

The benefits of this include: improved teaching and learning with an associated impact on standards; improved support for school leaders, giving them more time for strategic leadership; and the substantial expansion of the wider workforce at all levels, enabling schools to extend their curriculum and provide more care, guidance and support for pupils and thus better monitor their progress.

At its heart, the remodelling change management process is about successfully planning, developing and sustaining change in and across organizations and services. The process grew out of the commercial world and is highly transferable. It can be applied to any level of change and to any organization or group of organizations, large or small, public or commercial sector.

It helps organizations develop the additional flexibility, capacity and capability they need to successfully meet new challenges and requirements. It embeds a proactive and empowered culture by actively involving all staff in developing and implementing change and gives them the skills, experience, confidence and commitment to apply an effective remodelling approach to significant challenges into the long term.

Remodelling is enabling schools to establish high-quality extended services for the benefit of their pupils, parents and communities – such as childcare, breakfast and homework clubs, extra-curricular music and sports tuition, swift and easy access to additional support for vulnerable pupils, parenting support and community access to school facilities.

In addition, it is helping local areas – including local authorities, children's centres and a whole range of other organizations and agencies – countrywide to collaboratively reform and improve their targeted service support for young people by ensuring its delivery is more cohesive, coordinated and effective. In particular, it is helping create the cultural change necessary to ensure multi-agency working is both effective and personalized for the user.

This book is intended to support leaders and all other staff involved in organizational change – particularly, although far from exclusively, those working in the public sector. This includes senior managers in local authorities and other regional organizations, business leaders, politicians and government officials, heads of support services, lead practitioners, headteachers and other senior school employees, staff in public care trusts and other health care organizations, the police, youth justice, the voluntary and community sector and a whole range of other public and private organizations.

The core of this book describes the five distinct stages of the remodelling change process (and the way these stages embed a sustainable inclusive culture of continuous improvement) and the critical importance of collaborative change teams and leadership. The book begins by examining the global context of remodelling and follows this by looking at its history, starting from its beginnings in the commercial sector and following its successful progress up to its extensive current use in the public sector.

This book particularly draws on examples of remodelling in English public services and local government, as these services are currently under a great deal of pressure to reform and many of them – for example, schools, local authorities, children's centres and targeted youth support services – are actively working through the remodelling change process. The remodelling work of these organizations is directly applicable to other public organizations as well as the commercial sector in the UK and internationally.

Chapter 1 sets the global context for change and then focuses on the situation in the UK and, in particular, England. While the examples used tend to be drawn from schools and other organizations involved in the Every Child Matters agenda, the lessons that emerge are relevant to all other sectors. Every Child Matters is the UK government's vision of what, as a society, we want to achieve for our children.

Chapter 2 is more of an historical chapter drawing on the early days of remodelling and how it came about. It explains the background of remodelling, the reasons why it is seen as the way forward and its intellectual and commercial foundations.

Chapter 3 brings the story up to date. The focus is on the public sector, in particular, schools and other agencies and services that support children and young people. The work of these organizations is applicable to other organizations and sectors.

Chapter 4 outlines the remodelling process and Chapter 5 elaborates on the six key elements that ensure the process is effective.

Chapter 6 focuses on the role of change teams. These teams drive the remodelling process. They give all members of staff ownership of the changes that need to happen, they are the engine room of culture change and they encourage creativity and high team performance.

Chapter 7 concentrates on the leadership issues associated with remodelling. Remodelling creates a more devolved and inclusive culture where senior leaders still have a vital role and remain ultimate decision makers. The difference is that in remodelling organizations all staff groups, not only leaders, are fully involved in the creation and development of changes. Leaders often need to alter their style and learn new skills to facilitate this change.

The final chapter summarizes the learning from remodelling to date and looks to the future. Remodelling instils an inclusive, creative and flexible culture; an ongoing cycle of change. This culture is sustainable.

Acknowledgements

The remodelling change management process could not have become the powerful force for positive change it is today without the expertise, dedication and sheer determination of a very large group of people. And without all their hard work, and the phenomenal success of remodelling, this book would not have come into being.

This is why I want to start off by saying a huge and heartfelt thank you to all the thousands of individuals in schools and other public sector organizations who have worked, and are working, through the remodelling change process. By working inclusively and collaboratively, these people are transforming their own working lives and the effectiveness of their organizations and services and, even more importantly, improving outcomes for children and young people.

I must also give a very special thank you to two highly talented consultants and leaders, Malcolm Leith and Anthony Spooner, who left AT Kearney and KPMG in 2001 to form a new independent consultancy, Consulting Strategies Limited (CSL, now a part of Piscari Limited).

Malcolm and Anthony were instrumental in developing the remodelling change process and CSL was the driving force – in partnership with the London Leadership Centre – behind the National Remodelling Team (NRT), which first introduced and supported remodelling in all English schools and a range of other organizations. The NRT was originally part of the National College of School Leadership, before it amalgamated with the Teachers' Training Agency to form the Training and Development Agency for Schools (TDA) in 2006.

The NRT was somehow more than the sum of its parts; and its parts, although limited in number, were something extraordinary. It was an honour to lead and work with such a talented and creative team of consultants, regional advisors, technicians and writers.

These acknowledgements would certainly be incomplete without sending a special thank you to my deputy at the NRT, Howard Kennedy, an inspirational communicator and a tireless champion of remodelling. Howard now works as Director of Delivery in the TDA Executive Directorate for Development and Improvement.

I also want to thank TDA chief executive, Graham Holley, and the executive director of the EDDI, Hilary Emery, for their dedication and leadership, which is doing so much to improve the lives of children and young people, and their support for this book.

Another huge thank you must go to Tony Purcell and Neil del Strother, who have given me so much support and guidance in researching and editing this book. I would also like to thank Mike Lander and the Piscari Group for their encouragement and support. Without their help this book would not have been written.

A special word of thanks must go to the Social Partnership of department representatives, employers and unions who signed the remarkable workload agreement in 2003 that led to the formation of the NRT. Their unstinting support and challenge in the intervening years helped ensure the success of remodelling.

Finally, I would like to send an enormous thank you to a much (and all too often) underestimated group of wonderful and creative people – the children and young people of England. They are the reason I get up in the morning.

1 The imperative for change

At the heart of a learning organisation is a shift of mind – from seeing ourselves as separate from the world to connected to the world, from seeing problems as caused by something 'out there' to seeing how our own actions create the problems we experience. A learning organisation is a place where people are continually discovering how they create their reality and how they can change it.

(Senge, 2006, page 12)

Change is inevitable. It's happening all the time whether we acknowledge and welcome it or not. We all know this, of course; it is said so frequently it's almost a cliché. But even so, only too often we act as if it is not the case. Only too often we deny that any change is going on at all.

The result is that a great many of us are, at best, only passive participants in the changes we experience. We sit and impotently watch them unfolding around us, somehow believing there is little or nothing we can do to influence them. We hope that they will be for the best, rather than doing our utmost to direct them and *ensure* that they are for the best.

Essentially, we are relying on good fortune, rather than exercising our power to make sure that good and positive outcomes become our norm. This is how most of us approach even the least significant and most easily manageable changes in our lives. When we take this approach to the bigger changes and challenges we face, the consequences of this inaction are magnified.

Organizations

It is not only individuals, of course, who often take a largely passive approach to change. A great many organizations also put their proverbial heads in the sand and allow change to happen to them, blindly hoping that things will work out for the best or perhaps denying that it is happening at all.

This approach is, at best, flawed and, at worst, a complete disaster. It is abundantly clear that it makes more sense for organizations to plan for change, to welcome and relish it, and actively direct it in a way that leads to improved and sustained performance and a more conscious and collaborative approach to the work they do.

This is where the remodelling change process comes in. To put it simply, remodelling helps organizations direct and manage change – and so adapt, develop and succeed into the long term.

The way organizations perform – internationally, nationally and locally – impacts on us all. It not only has huge economic significance, it also influences our social and political structures. It is of crucial importance to all our lives, our present and our future. That is why – while it is not, of course, a panacea for all the world's problems and challenges – it is important to understand the urgent need for remodelling within the global context.

The global context

This is a time of profound and seismic global shifts. Our world is changing fundamentally; at an exhilarating, or terrifying and overwhelming (depending on your perspective) speed.

The changes and challenges we face today are even greater than those we faced (predominantly in the West) in the nineteenth century, when the industrial revolution exploded into being and fundamentally and permanently changed the way we work and live.

Today, the miracles and curses of the technological revolution are having a similar level of impact on our work and lives, only this time the change is even faster than in the eighteenth century and the impact is even more global and ubiquitous. Today, things are becoming possible, even commonplace, on a daily basis that only a few short years ago seemed like outlandish science fiction.

Faced with the scale of this change, the temptation to ignore it and carry on as we always have, or to believe we can do little or nothing at all to shape it, or to convince ourselves that it somehow has nothing to do with us, is perhaps greater than it has ever been in our history.

The technological revolution isn't happening in isolation of course. At the same time, the economies of the East are growing at an unprecedented pace, destabilizing the old economic status quo and creating uncertainty and conflict as well as opportunity: reserves of oil and other key resources are depleting at an alarming rate; our security is threatened by a real and sometimes over-imagined terrorist threat; and the earth itself is under dire environmental threat from our profligacy.

These momentous changes – and numerous others – are happening, here and now, whether we acknowledge them or do anything about them or not. They are affecting all our lives in a myriad of ways: political, economic, social, technical, legal, environmental ... you name it. And the stakes are higher than at any other time in our history.

What is important, in fact, what is vital, is that we take an active role and build and capitalize on these changes, directing and shaping them in a way that serves both us and the world. We *must* seize this opportunity.

Challenges

While desirable, directing and managing this level of global change is, of course, virtually – if not entirely – impossible. Change needs to take place at a local level, from a local perspective, and in manageable chunks. In many ways this is an echo of the 'think globally, act locally' rallying call of the late 60s.

The bedrock of local change is found in organizations. Our global economy is driven and underpinned by multinational, national and local companies. Our social structure, the way we operate, the way we live, is also fundamentally affected and reflected in the way these organizations operate.

It is not only commercial companies, of course, that have this effect. Our lives are also profoundly affected and reflected by the way public sector organizations – schools, hospitals, local authorities and local services – are organized. The role of these organizations is key.

One of the most immediate and pressing challenges shared by both public and private sector organizations, at least in the West, comes as a direct consequence of our ongoing technology and communications-driven shift from a manufacturing to a service-based economy.

These predictions help illustrate this shift:

- According to the Learning and Skills Council (2006), almost 50 per cent of jobs will require degree-level qualifications by 2014 (particularly in London where the 2006 level is 33 per cent).
- The UK Treasury is planning for 600,000 manual labour jobs in 2020, down from the present 4.6 million.
- *The Children's Plan* (DCSF, 2007a) sets targets for every young person to gain the skills for adult life and have access to further study, with at least 90 per cent achieving the equivalent of five higher-level GCSEs by the age of 19 (from 69 per cent in 2005), and at least 70 per cent achieving the equivalent of two A levels by the age of 19 by 2020. The Leitch Report (Leitch, 2006) recognizes that this will mean 1.9 million additional Level 3 attainments (A level or equivalent) over the period and boosting the number of apprentices to 500,000 a year.

This shift is fast making the old top-down organizational model that grew out of the industrial revolution a thing of the past. Today, inclusively and collaboratively involving all staff in all aspects of planning, production and delivery, and putting the customer at the heart of delivery (and often development), is becoming the norm.

Many organizations, both public and private, that are not responding and adapting to this change are already struggling as numerous leadership books and research studies indicate (several are quoted in the reference section of this book). These sources provide substantial evidence of organizational change that releases the capacity and capabilities of staff and stakeholders. See, for example, Jim Collins' publication *From Good to Great* (2001) and Margaret Wheatley's *Finding Our Way: Leadership For an Uncertain Time* (2007).

In addition to this shift, and supportive of it, are hundreds of other changes and challenges, many of them occurring and impacting at both a global and local level. This is changing the way organizations operate in all sorts of new ways. At the core of all this change is workforce development.

The movement to greater personalization is not only customer facing, it is also an internal process. A strong focus on individuals, both customers and staff, is becoming more and more important to success. To do this effectively, organizations need to become more demand led, reforming their staffing models and making them more inclusive and flexible. The following points illustrate the need for workforce deveopment:

- Intellectual capital (and those that hold it) has become one of organizations' most valuable resources, if not the most valuable. This gives employees a great deal more power, importance and influence than they have ever previously had.
- The increasing mobility of all levels of workers, added to the importance of intellectual capital, is dramatically changing the way employees are viewed and treated.
- The nature of leadership is changing, from the 'hero' leader of old to a more democratic, inclusive and collaborative model.
- Organizations are looking more and more to develop new collaborative partnerships (locally, nationally and internationally), often supported by the efficiencies and capabilities of new technology, to enhance their work.
- The speed of change is increasing and this demands correspondingly flexible organizations – with flexible and talented staff – that are able to adapt and change equally quickly.
- Ongoing training and continual professional development for staff, i.e. a high level of staff expertise, is becoming increasingly key to organizations' long-term success.

These changes are not news. In fact, many of our more forward thinking organizations have already addressed them head on – and continue to address them. For example, in England, our schools, local authorities and range of support agencies and other organizations, have used and continue to use the remodelling change process to direct, manage and adapt to these changes in a successful and sustainable way.

This is not true, though, for the majority of organizations – public and private. A recent IBM survey *Unlocking the DNA of the Adaptable Workforce: The Global Human Capital Study* (2007) found that many companies have yet to make all the necessary changes, i.e. 'only 14 percent of the companies surveyed believe their workforce is very capable of adapting to change'.

Unlocking the DNA of the adaptable workforce

IBM interviewed 400 major companies in 40 countries around the world for its survey. Its aim was twofold: to understand how these organizations are improving the performance of their workforce to compete more effectively and to identify leading practices and opportunities for organizations to improve their overall workforce performance.

The survey reports that enhancing workforce performance requires four key components: an adaptable workforce that can rapidly respond to changes in the outside market; effective leadership to guide individuals through change and deliver results; an integrated talent management model that addresses the entire employee lifecycle; workforce analytics that can deliver strategic insight and measure success.

- *Adaptable workforce*: the companies that were interviewed listed the many forces that are driving the need for organizations to develop a workforce able to rapidly adapt to changing external conditions, such as: globalization, market volatility, security concerns, changing demographics, global competition and new business models.

  The survey adds that organizations looking to improve their workforce adaptability should focus on three areas: creating a formal process to predict the anticipated demand for skills needed to deliver on strategy; developing expertise that combines skills management with employee profiles and social networking technologies; encouraging collaboration through performance measures and communities, and embedding collaborative technologies into day-to-day processes.
- *Effective leadership*: the survey also uncovered a general concern among companies about a shortage of individuals who can: provide leadership, guide people through change and drive and deliver results. The companies surveyed were 'clearly concerned with their current and future leadership capability' and aware that developing leaders involves more than simply 'dipping' people into executive education courses.
- *Talent management*: the surveyed companies saw talent management as a potential risk area. A probable higher turnover of staff will affect many companies and, to succeed (and ensure talent is nurtured, developed and maintained), they need to focus on the entire employee lifecycle.

- *Workforce analytics*: companies in the survey talked about the need to develop workforce analytics that deliver strategic insights, contribute to business strategy and help assess and measure success – and so help drive future changes and future success. There was a general awareness that getting this right is not always easy.

The level and depth of these changes requires more from organizations – both public and private – than just a gentle prune of the far branches of the way they work, it requires them to dig down deep and change their core structure – increasing their capacity and transforming the whole way they operate.

Changing organizations

Public and private sector organizations both have the power – and a responsibility – to lead and manage this change. In fact, to adapt to and capitalize on the extraordinary global and local changes that are taking place, they simply have to change to survive (and thrive). In other words, change is not an option.

Change is a necessity; and to succeed it is vital that organizations direct change in a well-planned and structured way that builds on existing good practice and adapts to global and local challenges. They must ensure that all staff are involved in developing positive, effective and sustainable solutions that encompass the need for an adaptable workforce, effective leadership, talent management and workforce analytics.

To do this successfully, organizations need to employ a structured approach to change that is able to cope with, and develop and direct all the complex and interdependent facets of change – rational, political and emotional – of the early twenty-first century.

One structured approach to change is remodelling. This change process takes organizations through five distinct, often overlapping, stages (explained in detail in Chapter 4). Each stage comes with a set of change tools and activities developed and tailored to fit each individual organization's – or group of organizations' – requirements and aims.

Organizations typically follow an emotional change curve (see Chapter 4 for detail) when they redesign and restructure the way they operate. The remodelling change process is built around this curve and provides the right support at the right time to ensure organizations cope well with the ups and particularly the downs of change.

An important outcome of working through each of the five stages of the remodelling change process is an implicit sixth stage: sustainability. To ensure sustainability, remodelling solutions need to be designed and implemented in a way that allows them to evolve flexibly, as and when necessary.

The remodelling change process builds, whever possible, on existing good practice. It achieves flexibility by embedding an underlying culture of active collaboration, inclusiveness, staff empowerment, and continual assessment and refinement of solutions and services. It brings out the inherent creativity that exists in every human being.

And, arguably, nowhere is the need for this more evident and necessary than in the public sector.

The public sector

Public sector organiszations help form and are formed by the way we live and work. Many of these organizations are directly connected to government and effectively operate as the practical delivery end of government policy (as well as also often feeding back information to government from the 'front line'). Others, for example, many voluntary and community organizations, have no immediate connection to government. Either way, all public sector organizations play some sort of a role in shaping our present and our future.

As mentioned, public services share many of the same challenges as the business sector, not least the need to become more personalized and less centralized, more 'bottom-up', and more service and customer led. If anything, the challenges in the public sector tend to be even more entrenched and ubiquitous than in the business sector, as the public sector has generally not had to develop under quite such an unforgiving commercial spotlight as most businesses and so can lack the efficiencies this encourages.

The public sector also faces a range of other drivers for change not generally faced by the commercial sector, for example: top-down directives and regulations from Westminster (in England) and from the European Union, including government efficiency targets (often developed in response to public opposition to tax and spend); instructions from Westminster and Brussels around creating more local control of public services; increased service user expectation; increased service user sophistication; a realization that one size doesn't fit all; pressure from public service unions and local democratic bodies; the increasingly changing role of local authorities and the health service (and their equivalents) from pure service providers towards a commissioning role; and new partnerships between the public sector, the private sector and the voluntary and community sector.

The 2006 report, *Prosperity for All in the Global Economy – world class skills*, commissioned by the UK Treasury and undertaken by Lord Leitch, states that:

> . . . despite substantial investment and reform plans already in place, by 2020, we will have managed only to 'run to stand still'. On our current trajectory, the UK's comparative position will not have improved significantly. In the meantime, the world will have continued to change and the global environment will be even harsher. The scale of the challenge is daunting.
>
> Our recommendations start with an ambitious vision. The UK must become a world leader in skills. [This is] the most important lever within our control to create wealth and to reduce social deprivation. (page 2)

The report goes on to recommend:

> . . . a simplified demand-led system with employers and individuals having a strong and coherent voice. The Review recommends that all publicly funded, adult vocational skills in England, apart from community learning, go through demand-led routes by 2010. This means all adult skills funding should be routed through Train to Gain and Learner Accounts by 2010. The switch to demand-led funding and end to the supply-side planning of adult skills provision fundamentally changes the role planning bodies, such as the LSC, which will require further significant streamlining. (page 138)

The pressing need for reform in English public services is not just due to the global, national and local factors discussed earlier in this chapter. The goal of social equity, in particular, remains a driving force, in England, behind this need.

A recent study by the Sutton Trust (Blanden and Machin, 2007) states that:

> There is no evidence that these relationships have changed in a consistent way over this period. This is in stark contrast with the strengthening relationship between intermediate outcomes and parental income that accompanied the previously well documented decline in social mobility that occurred for birth cohorts from 1958 and 1970. Our findings suggest that the decline in intergenerational mobility that occurred between these cohorts is not ongoing, but neither has there been any significant improvement. (page 1)

One of the studies key findings, replicated in earlier research, was equally alarming:

> Those from the poorest fifth of households but in the brightest group drop from the 88th percentile on cognitive tests at age three to the 65th percentile at age five. Those from the richest households who are least able at age three move up from the 15th percentile to the 45th percentile by age five. If this trend were to continue, the children from affluent backgrounds would be likely to overtake the poorer children in test scores by age seven. (Sutton Trust, December, 2007, Summary)

Similar evidence has been produced in studies undertaken by the Centre for Longitudinal Studies, based at the Institute of Education, University of London (see Figure 1.1).

To work towards the goal of social equity, public services have to respond and adapt to the great social and economic shifts that have taken place in England over the last 20 or 30 years. For example: the increase in and redistribution of wealth (the rich have got richer, many of the poor are worse off in relative terms); the growing perception of a lack of social cohesion with continuing concerns over the growth in immigration; the ostracization of Muslims in some communities; the changing nature of family structure;

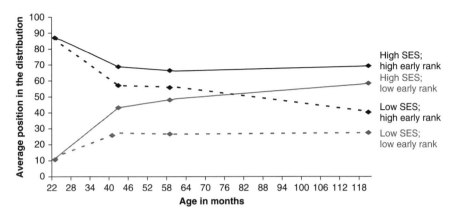

Figure 1.1 Attainment according to social economic status of the young (Feinstein, 2003).

growing financial instability, the reduction in social housing stock; and the changing model of employment – where outsourcing manual, skilled and semi-skilled jobs that used to be in the public sector (where people felt more of a sense of ownership) to external providers is now the norm.

Social cohesion was one of the government's three core priorities when it came to power in 1997. The Local Government White Paper, *Strong and Prosperous Communities* (DCLG, 2006), reiterated this aim in one of its eight guiding principles:

> Visible work to tackle inequalities provides a strong foundation for cohesion. Communities who experience unequal life chances or who experience discrimination and prejudice are less likely to connect to, or feel part of a wider society. Poor schools and health services, or a lack of skills training and employment opportunities, are factors which blight any community. They cause people to lose faith in public services and in authorities more generally. They corrode trust between communities. A commitment to social cohesion has to have building a fair and more equal society at its heart. (Volume 1, pages 158–9)

All of the above factors, and many others not mentioned, add up to a burning platform for change – and for developing the capability and capacity to lead and manage change – in English public services. This is well recognized and understood by central and local government.

In response, local authorities and regional government offices are increasingly taking a more proactive approach to change, using the remodelling process to incorporate, for example, more individual and personalized local and regional targets into their local area agreements, which in turn inform their Joint Area Reviews and Annual Performance Assessments.

Education

Perhaps the greatest impact of remodelling, to date, is being felt in our schools, where the process has become a well-established way to approach, lead and manage change. Schools started working with the process in 2003, to help them implement the requirements of the National Agreement, and have continued using it as a way of creating the capacity they need to develop extended services. This is already reaping a range of very positive results and an increase in standards.

Children who entered school in 2008 will almost certainly be in compulsory education or training until at least 2021 and, for the majority, it is likely that their formal education will continue beyond that time – at university or in some other type of further education. We cannot assume that even this generation will enjoy the same privileges during its adult life as many of us in England have enjoyed since the middle of the twentieth century, let alone those that follow.

The same thing, of course, but with different dates, could have been said about any cohort of children during any modern age. But, as mentioned previously, the changes we are now experiencing at a global level – with a corresponding knock-on effect at a national and local level – are unprecedented. And that means that today's children, and schools, are facing unprecedented challenges.

For better or for worse, schools are in many ways a political weather vane, or perhaps more accurately a testing ground, for change. You only have to witness New Labour's focus on 'education, education, education' to know this.

This focus on education has spawned, and continues to spawn, a huge variety of government policies and directives aimed to improve our schools and the outcomes for children and young people. There is an understandable urgency about ensuring our children and young people have the support and skills they need to survive and do well in the new world we are creating.

A high-profile example of government policy aimed directly at improving outcomes for young people is the Green Paper *Every Child Matters* (HM Treasury, 2003), followed by *Every Child Matters: Change for Children* (DfES, 2004) and a series of associated documents targeted at schools and a range of relevant services, including health, social services and youth justice. *The Children's Plan* (DCSF, 2007a) builds on this agenda and sets out a vision and programme for children over the next ten years.

Every Child Matters is a new approach to the well-being of children and young people from birth to age 19. The government's aim is for all children, whatever their background or circumstances, to have the support they need to: be healthy, stay safe, enjoy and achieve, make a positive contribution to society and achieve economic wellbeing.

This means that all organizations involved with providing services to children, particularly schools, need to work and collaborate in new ways – sharing information and working together to protect children and young people from harm and help them achieve what they want in life.

Other recent government directives and policies that impact on schools address issues as diverse as looked-after children, inclusion, personalized learning, disability, travellers, cultural diversity, nationality, things to do/places to go, targeted youth support and teacher workload.

For example, the *Care Matters: Time for Change* (DfES, 2007) White Paper sets out a new commitment to looked-after children. It promises them new educational opportunities to ensure that they are enabled and empowered to have better opportunities in later life. Schools are one of the many organizations affected by this and the subsequent Children and Young People's Bill (2008).

Other examples include: the 2007 Children's Plan's focus on the importance of the Early Years Foundation Programme, the personalized learning agenda and the 14 to 19 Curriculum Strategy. All of these agendas require proactive change management if they are to be implemented successfully and cohesively.

However well thought through these government policies and directives may be, they inevitably, at least initially, put pressure on schools and local areas as they work to interpret and implement them. There has also been an historical problem that many policies and directives have come through piecemeal, i.e., they haven't been joined up into any sort of cohesive or understandable strategy. This put a huge stress on schools that, in many cases, had already been struggling with resources to simply carry out their core education role.

The recent creation of the Department for Children, Schools and Families (DCSF) represents a sign of the increasing government commitment to ensure joined up strategy, planning and delivery. Other recent strong evidence of the government's commitment includes *The Children's Plan* (DCSF, 2007a). Since the publication of *The Children's Plan* the DCSF has published *Building Brighter Futures: Next Steps for the Children's Workforce* (2008), which describes the actions that will be taken to further improve the skills and capacity of people who work with children to deliver the high quality, personalized and integrated services described in *The Children's Plan*.

If organizations and services dealing with children and young people are to lead and manage the scale of modernization required, they need an effective process to make it a reality. Remodelling is this process. It builds on the creativity of all staff and stakeholders to bring about substantial, beneficial and sustainable change.

2 Remodelling: the early days

When you are inspired by some great purpose, some extraordinary project, all your thoughts break their bounds: your mind transcends limitations, your consciousness expands in every direction, and you find yourself in a new, great, and wonderful world. Dormant forces, faculties, and talents become alive, and you discover yourself to be a greater person by far than you ever dreamed yourself to be.

(Patanjali, philosopher, 200 BC)

Remodelling is a unique, creative, coherent and highly effective change management process that can be adapted to virtually any change situation. While rigour and demanding standards underpin its design, it is not influenced by any one single intellectual, theoretical or historical approach.

The process incorporates the most effective parts of a range of change processes deployed over recent years by consultancies in the commercial sector. It has evolved, and continues to evolve, predominantly through practical application.

This chapter and Chapter 3 give an overview of the history of the remodelling change process, describing how it has evolved – and its impact – to date. The mechanics of the remodelling process itself are described in detail in Chapters 4 and 5.

Early days

Remodelling first appeared as a coherent change management process in the early 1990s. The change process was developed in the commercial sector to help companies successfully achieve the complex strategic and structural changes necessary to meet the many new challenges of the technological age.

A wide range of existing change management processes was examined to find out which techniques and approaches worked best. The change process that evolved from this work was most heavily based on the work of W. Edwards Deming and Joseph M. Duran, the founders of total quality management (TQM).

TQM is a management strategy aimed at embedding the awareness of quality in all organizational processes. It has been widely used in manufacturing, education, government and service industries, as well as NASA space and science programmes. It heavily influenced the team-based organizational change movement.

Over time and through the movement of employees, a powerful version of the now proven change process found its way to KPMG (a major management consultancy). KPMG developed and honed the new change process in the most practical way possible – through using it to support a number of the UK's most influential companies' move from struggling to cope with change to leading and shaping it.

The remodelling process developed quickly as a result. In particular, it developed through helping these companies to fundamentally transform their working processes and cultures to meet the demands imposed by the requirements of the knowledge age, the move to personalization and the pressures of globalization.

Remodelling enabled these companies to embrace and lead change rather than simply cope with it. It helped them develop the additional flexibility, capacity and capability to successfully meet new challenges and requirements into the long term. In short, the remodelling process proved itself by enabling these companies to make the necessary cultural and structural developments to manage and succeed in a rapidly changing business world.

Academic rigour

In addition to evolving through practical application, the remodelling change process also developed through integrating insights, understandings and benefits gained from a broad swathe of academic research.

This includes work on: experiential learning (David Kolb, 1984); double-loop and organizational learning (Chris Argyris, 1999); systems thinking (Peter Senge, 2006); emotional intelligence (Daniel Goleman, 2004, 2007); why leadership and change agendas often fail (John Kotter, 1996, 2002); and school leadership in a culture of change (Michael Fullan, 2001, 2003).

In addition, remodelling also draws on diverse and seminal work on: teamworking (Peter Scholtes, 1998); the rational, political and emotional aspects of change (Daryl Conner, 1993); stakeholder management and organizational transition (Richard Beckhard and Reuben Harris, 1987); the emotional change curve around death and dying (Elizabeth Kubler-Ross, 1997); cultural change (Ed Schein, 2004); and productive workplaces (Marvin Weisbord and Sandra Janoff, 1995).

As its reputation spreads and its impact becomes more and more evident, remodelling is increasingly also becoming the *subject* of academic work. For example, it is featured in books by: Sara Bubb and Peter Earley (2004) from the Institute of Education; and Sonia Blandford (2005) from Canterbury Christ Church University.

Evaluation reports also point to the positive impact of remodelling. For example, the National Foundation for Educational Research's (NFER) evaluation reports that the majority of schools it surveyed considered that the remodelling process was 'fit for purpose and provided enough flexibility to be adapted to the needs of the local setting. We aim to make school leaders and staff believe' (Easton *et al.*, 2006, page x).

In addition, as mentioned in the introduction to this book, Ofsted's 2007 report, *Reforming and Developing the School Workforce*, states that remodelling has led to 'a revolutionary shift in workforce culture' (page 6) in schools.

CSL

The remodelling process moved and evolved once again when two senior former KPMG change consultants formed a new independent consultancy – Consulting Strategies Limited (CSL) – in 2001.

Shortly after its foundation, CSL was invited by the London Leadership Centre (at the Institute of Education, University of London) to form a consortium to bid for the Transforming the School Workforce Pathfinder (TSWP). The TSWP contract was put out to tender by the Department for Education and Skills (DfES), now the DCSF.

TSWP

The rationale behind the one-year TSWP pathfinder was the growing awareness that teachers were working excessively long hours in schools. Teaching unions and the DfES both shared the view that teacher workload was becoming – in many cases had already become – unmanageable (NB workload was the major reason cited by teachers for leaving the profession), and that teacher wellbeing and school standards were suffering as a result.

This awareness was given extra substance by evidence from a government-commissioned report, carried out by PricewaterhouseCoopers in 2001, which revealed that:

- Teachers were working around 52 hours per week during term time.
- Teachers and headteachers were working more intensive weeks than comparable professionals and managers in other professions.
- Teachers undertook tasks which they did not believe were necessary to support teaching.
- The pace and manner of change in schools was working against achieving high standards.

Schools were also facing a range of other issues that were impacting on standards of teaching and learning. These included:

- More than 30 per cent of teachers' work time was spent on non-teaching activities.
- Teachers generally had a poor work/life balance.
- One in five newly qualified teachers were leaving the profession before they reached their fourth year of teaching.
- There was a need for the development of more professional support staff.
- There were specific teacher shortages in a number of key subjects.

In addition, a range of other more 'macro' factors – including social and technological changes, employment legislation, government initiatives and new models of learning and pupil assessment – were all driving change at breakneck speed and adding to school workload and a growing sense of chaos and diminishing morale.

It was clear to all involved that the issues schools were facing needed addressing urgently if the government was going to make a lasting impact on the cycle of under-achievement in England.

Structured change process

The London Leadership Centre Consortium won the TSWP contract. The primary aim of the pathfinder, which ran for a year in 32 schools from September 2002, was to test, explore and learn as much as possible about implementing workforce reform in schools.

The pathfinder called for a structured change process to help the 32 schools build the capacity and capability they needed to implement and embrace workforce reform. The consortium developed the remodelling change process, with its five distinct stages, specifically for schools.

From the start, there was a clear awareness that remodelling provided the opportunity and method to enable schools to focus on the way they worked and assess the roles of all involved in the education of their pupils – with an aim to improve teaching and learning and provide every pupil with a chance to achieve greater success and higher standards.

Cultural change

Rather than just being a set of instructions to follow, the process involved a fundamental alteration in the cultural mindset of many schools as it involved schools moving from a, only too often, traditional top-down management model to a more inclusive model (involving the whole school workforce in decision making).

If you involve people in decisions about change they are not afraid of it. (Marian Catterall, headteacher, North Manchester School for Girls)

The essential elements of the version of the remodelling change process that was specifically adapted for schools included (NB. these elements, in some form, help underpin the remodelling change process in all environments):

- The recognition that one size does not fit all – change is an individual school-based process.
- The vital importance of addressing the emotional and political aspects of change as well as the rational.
- Establishing a compelling reason for change, a clear vision of the future and a coherent plan for getting there. Sustainable change depends on these three factors.
- Working through all five stages of the remodelling process, i.e. not skipping any.
- Understanding, valuing and acting on what people involved in change are thinking, doing, feeling and saying at each stage of the change process.
- A recognition that people go through an emotional change curve and that this is not necessarily a straightforward journey.
- The use of external, objective support and challenge.
- Teamwork – through the use of school change teams representing all school staff.

Change teams are a key part of successful remodelling in schools, as they are in all successful remodelling, both in the public and the commercial sector. In schools, change teams were set up right at the start of the remodelling change process to provide leadership for the change programme. They are made up of representatives of the whole school workforce, including teachers, support staff, administration staff, governors – and often parents, pupils and local organizations.

Change teams look different in each school in terms of composition, how and when they meet, the roles of people on the team, the time commitments team members make, and so on. What is vital is that they are fully inclusive, as this ensures all viewpoints and ideas are considered and because people support what they help to create – and broad involvement leads to better and more lasting improvement.

As previously mentioned, all the school staff groups are involved in school change teams. Representatives of these different groups bring their own, and their colleagues', views and issues around workload to the change team meetings and contribute on a constructive basis. They act as a two-way communications channel on an ongoing basis with their colleagues, ensuring all views and ideas are heard and included throughout the change process.

Remodelling change teams are discussed at greater length in the next chapter and in Chapter 6.

Impact

The 32 schools involved in the pathfinder reported significant results; in particular: a growing awareness of the potential of the remodelling change process to improve educational standards; improved and improving teaching staff attitudes towards the contribution made by support staff; and, most significantly, a real reduction in teachers' working hours.

Primary school deputies, for example, reported an average reduction in working time of over seven hours a week and teaching staff in primary and secondary special schools were working on average four hours fewer each week.

Pathfinder case study: Horton Lodge School (63 pupils, community special primary, Staffordshire)

Horton Lodge is a Key Learning Centre, catering for children with physical disabilities and also provides support for up to 100 mainstream schools on inclusion issues. The school needed a staffing structure to reflect the necessity for a differentiated and active learning approach for pupils.

To implement this, a number of key appointments was made, including professional support workers, a resource manager and an administrative support manager. Support staff have been given training and during STAR week, when teachers set targets and carry out assessment and recording, support staff lead in the classrooms.

Teacher workload has been reduced by around four hours a week, support staff contribute more fully to pupils' education and the school reports that pupil learning opportunities have improved.

The pathfinder also helped teaching staff to realize the potential of information and communications technology (ICT) to have a positive impact on workload and teaching and learning, with all of the pathfinder schools reporting an increase in their use of ICT coupled with teachers reporting higher levels of job satisfaction.

The pathfinder schools found they required more distributed leadership and delegation to achieve their goals. School remodelling change teams were seen as being very effective in delivering this. Support staff were especially positive about being included in change teams.

Overall, working through the remodelling change process helped the pathfinder schools move significantly towards ensuring that:

- teaching and learning is their main focus;
- all of their workforce is involved in making decisions;

- non-teaching tasks and activities are undertaken by appropriate people within flexible working patterns;
- managing change is a normal part of school life;
- the school shares experiences and learning with other schools;
- the staff work/life balance is acceptable to the whole workforce;
- all of the school workforce and other stakeholders are aware of the direction of the school.

Pathfinder case study: Lydbury North Church of England School (37 pupils, primary, Shropshire)

As a small rural primary school, many issues at Lydbury North centred around isolation and coping with very limited staffing resources. To tackle these, the school formed part of a cluster, with the aim of improving collaboration and communication between the neighbouring schools. New teaching assistants have enabled teachers to focus on teaching and learning, and the secretary's role was enhanced to relieve teaching staff of more administrative tasks. The schools have used modern communications technology to improve connectivity between them and have organized days where pupils from the various schools meet up. Joint school development planning is enabling the schools to share ideas and consultancy costs. The schools plan to increase connectivity by improving their ICT infrastructure.

Making changes and implementing solutions inevitably provokes emotional and political responses from those involved and affected. For example, transferring administrative tasks from teachers to support staff in the pathfinder often caused some initial anxiety. A common reaction was to say 'It's not easy to abandon things which we've always done like that and embrace a new way of working.' Another consideration was a need for appropriate remuneration for new support staff with new responsibilities.

Key to overcoming these and other barriers to change was involving the whole workforce and the wider community in the change process – collaboratively looking at the issues and developing a shared, clear vision and an agreed way forward. The remodelling change process enabled schools to do this. These changes were not limited to the schools in the pathfinder. Several of the consultants who supported the process were serving headteachers and they took the process and the learning back into their own schools.

As more and more evidence was collected of a quiet revolution taking place in schools, the realization began to dawn that not only was remodelling achievable, but that it represented perhaps the most powerful tool we have for changing the education landscape.

Remodelling is a fundamental departure from the many top-down initiatives schools have become used to over the years. In fact, the pathfinder schools reported that remodelling was the glue that helped bind all these initiatives together; enabling them to develop their own tailored solutions and helping them to change and develop in a coherent and joined-up way

The Radclyffe School in Oldham (2008) was one of the original pathfinders and continues to use remodelling to lead and manage change. Headteacher Hardial Hayer explains why: 'I want us to look at innovative ways of working without compromising our number one objective of raising standards.'

In a letter to parents he reiterates this commitment:

> At the Radclyffe School our aim is to provide the widest educational opportunity to all our students, that is, extending the most able and challenging and stretching the less able and less well-motivated students. In other words, we want every individual child to achieve personal excellence. We want our school to be a first class place of learning and a caring community, where children feel happy and secure and where the emphasis is on achievement. (Radclyffe School, 2008)

Since 2003 5+ A* to Cs at GCSE have risen at Radclyffe from 31 per cent to 69 per cent. At the same time, GCSE results, including English and maths, have more than doubled, going from 23 per cent to 47 per cent. Deputy headteacher Mark Fowle explains the impact of the first school remodelling change plan devised by the school change team (SCT):

> The draft school change plan (SCP) consisted of three key proposals, reflecting the areas prioritized at the launch evening. These were: a capital build project to construct a cover and communication area which would address the issues of communication and workload, and protect staff non-contact time; the appointment of non-teacher year managers and six faculty support assistants (FSAs), the cost of which would be met partly by point holders giving up one non-contact lesson per week; and the purchase of a laptop for each member of staff, the set up of a radio link and the appointment of network manager.

> The draft SCP was presented to staff at a whole school training day where each strand was discussed in clusters chaired by a member of the SCT. It got a mixed reaction. Some staff were enthusiastic about the prospect of change. Others felt anxious and threatened, so the SCP was amended to accommodate some of their concerns. The final plan only requested two year managers to replace two vacant head of year positions. Also, only two FSAs were requested as some faculties disagreed with the idea of giving up non-contact time. (TDA remodelling case study, 2003)

A national agreement

While the TSWP pathfinder was in progress, the government drew up the agreement: *Raising Standards, Tackling Workload: a national agreement* (The Social Partnership, 2003) – co-created and signed by a unique social partnership of government, employers and school workforce unions on 15 January 2003.

The signatories were the Department for Education and Skills (DfES) (now the DCSF), the Welsh Assembly, teachers' unions and professional associations including: the Association of Teachers and Lecturers (ATL), the National Association of Headteachers (NAHT), the National Association of Schoolmasters and Union of Women Teachers (NASUWT), the Professional Association of Teachers (PAT, now Voice), and the Secondary Headteachers' Association (SHA, now the Association of School and College Leaders), and support staff unions including the Britain's General Union (GMB), the Transport and General Workers' Union (T&G, now Unite), Unison and representatives of the Employers' Organisation through the National Employers' Organisation for School Teachers (NEOST).

The agreement, which was subsequently incorporated into the School Teachers' Pay and Conditions Document, has dramatically changed many school teachers' working lives and opened up new opportunities for support staff.

The remodelling change process, which had been further refined for use in the education sector during the TSWP year, was written into the National Agreement for the roll-out contract (awarded to the newly formed National Remodelling Team (NRT) – an extension of the London Leadership Centre Consortium under the management of NCSL) for all England.

The Workforce Agreement Monitoring Group (WAMG), which is made up of representatives of the signatories of the National Agreement, was charged with: finalizing the contractual and legal framework for the agreement; overseeing the implementation of the agreement; and initiating change on the ground by providing guidance and support to schools and local authorities.

The National Agreement acknowledged the pressure on schools to raise standards and set out a plan to tackle unacceptable workload levels for teachers. It introduced a series of significant changes to teachers' conditions of service, introduced in three annual phases from September 2003.

The three phases of contractual changes arising from the agreement for teachers were:

- 1 September 2003: routine delegation of administrative and clerical tasks; introduction of work/life balance clauses, and the introduction of leadership and management time for those with corresponding responsibilities.

- 1 September 2004: the introduction of new limits on covering for absent colleagues (38 hours per year).
- 1 September 2005: the introduction of guaranteed professional time for planning, preparation and assessment (PPA); the introduction of dedicated headship time and the introduction of new invigilation arrangements.

Significantly, the National Agreement did not focus solely on teachers. It also acknowledged the vital role played by school support staff, which led directly to the establishment of higher level teaching assistant (HLTA) standards and the certificate in school business management (CSBM). The agreement has also helped create other new roles in schools for adults who support teachers' work and pupils' learning.

The NRT

The success of the pathfinder led to the establishment, in April 2003, of the NRT, to support and lead the roll-out of the National Agreement. The NRT was a major expansion of the London Leadership Centre Consortium, and brought in local authorities and local WAMG groups to help deliver the remodelling change process at a local level.

The NRT, which was initially hosted within the NCSL, worked in partnership with local authorities, remodelling consultants, regional centres, national WAMG and the DfES.

During its three years of leading the roll-out of the national agreement, the NRT also worked closely with a range of other organizations involved in the education sector, such as the TTA (now the Training and Development Agency for Schools – TDA), Ofsted and governor associations.

The primary aim of the NRT was very clear: to improve educational outcomes for pupils. As the author said at the launch speech of the NRT (Collarbone, 2003):

> We aim to make school leaders and staff believe that change can and will occur, and that, working together, they have the power to make it happen. Teachers will focus more on teaching and learning, supported by other adults as part of a whole school team. The greatest beneficiaries will be the pupils, who will have more individualized attention enabling them to realise full and productive lives. This is the future and we are creating it together.

The roll-out

Over a three-year period, starting in 2003, the NRT worked closely with local authorities to take all 23,000 plus schools in England through the remodelling change process.

It was not feasible for all 23,000 schools to start the remodelling process at the same time, as the NRT consisted, at the start of the roll-out, of only 15 employees (this grew to around 80 staff by the end of the three years). To ensure all schools got the hands-on support they required, local authorities assigned their schools to three staggered remodelling waves (or tranches).

These tranches were supported throughout the remodelling process by regional events organized by the NRT and local authorities. The NRT trained and supported a large number of local authority remodelling advisers to help with these events and to give support to individual schools. A key role of the advisers was mobilizing their local authorities to deliver the remodelling change process successfully. To do this, they:

- ensured the necessary resources existed within each region to support the roll-out;
- ran launch and regional events for participating schools;
- visited schools at various stages throughout their remodelling journeys to provide support and challenge;
- championed best practice and encouraged collaboration between schools.

Each school worked through the five stages of the remodelling change process over a six- to nine-month period – moving from initially identifying and exploring the issues to developing solutions and delivering results.

> ### Remodelling case study: Ellowes Hall Secondary School (1,100 pupils, mixed secondary, Dudley)
>
> Workforce reform at Ellowes Hall began with a review of current practice to link staff tasks to school objectives. As a result of the remodelling process, administrative and support staff now see their work as more connected with teaching and learning. Learning support assistants, in particular, have a strong engagement with the learning outcomes of the class. To address teacher workload, vertical year groups were introduced to spread pressure points over the year – this gives pupils more attention during difficult times and spreads out the teachers' workload, particularly with regard to parental contact.
>
> Since 2003 the schools 5+ A* to C results have improved from 33 per cent to 56 per cent but, perhaps more spectacularly, results including English and maths have improved every year from 26 per cent in 2003 to 43 per cent in 2007.

The schools' use of remodelling didn't stop there though. Working through the remodelling change process inevitably facilitates a change of culture, where all staff become involved in collaboratively addressing challenges and developing solutions on an ongoing basis. In short, remodelling schools continue remodelling – and using the change process to manage change becomes a normal and welcome part of school life.

Exceeding targets

The NRT consistently exceeded its targets for the roll-out. The primary reason for this was the effectiveness of the remodelling change process. NRT consultants were also instrumental in this success. They tirelessly travelled the country facilitating workshops and other events that supported schools in making the most of remodelling.

In the first year of the roll-out, the NRT almost doubled its target of engaging 1,300 schools in the change process. It also easily exceeded its target of engaging 50 per cent of schools by mid-2005.

By the end of 2006, as ambitiously planned, virtually every school in England was implementing the national agreement. For the first time ever, representatives of all school staff were working together in proactive change teams, addressing challenges collaboratively and developing made-to-measure solutions targeted at making long-term and sustainable improvements in their schools.

> ## Remodelling case study: Penryn College (860 pupils, comprehensive, secondary, community sports college, Cornwall)
>
> As a school in a deprived area, with 25 per cent special needs, it was not surprising that the school's remodelling change team identified a need to promote student achievement. Systems were set up to promote sharing best practice and a scheme was introduced to encourage staff to submit school improvement ideas. Staff agreed that pupil behaviour was a major issue and a review of the pastoral system resulted in the introduction of vertical tutor groups, peer mentoring and a behaviour support unit. To involve the pupils in their own learning, a survey was carried out to gauge their opinions of the school. Results revealed a desire for 'less chalk and talk' and pupils got involved in putting together an action plan to implement this.

Financial management

The demands of the national agreement highlighted the need for improved financial management in many schools. Their mindset was very much that change meant spending money and, as remodelling and the requirement to implement the national agreement did not come with significant funding, this mindset needed to change.

In the commercial sector, of course, making performance improvements does not necessarily mean spending more money. In fact, it generally means quite the reverse as improved performance often comes through making efficiencies and streamlining processes.

The remodelling change process was adapted to help schools successfully improve their financial management. In parallel with the roll-out of the national agreement, the NRT was asked by the Secretary of State to set up a new workstream – Financial Management in Schools (FMiS, 2008). The aim of FMiS was to help the most in need schools and local authorities use remodelling to investigate and improve their financial management.

The remodelling change programme was tailored to help schools address their financial issues. Working in partnership with education consultants from KPMG, the NRT helped around one-third of all schools in England to improve their financial management (between September 2003 and March 2004).

At this time, the Financial Management Standards in Schools (FMSiS) were being developed by the Institute of Public Finance (IPF), on behalf of the DfES. The NRT drew widely on this work to help develop its support programme. Much of this work now forms part of the NCSL school business management programme. Visit www.ncsl.org.uk/fmis-index for details.

By early 2004, the success of remodelling had made it clear that it provided an excellent method to develop and implement the government's public sector change agenda. The next chapter looks at this in detail.

3 Remodelling: extending the agenda

A journey of a thousand miles must begin with a single step.

(Lao Tzu, Chinese philosopher, c. 614–513 BC)

Remodelling enables organizations to successfully address and lead change. Crucially it does this in an inclusive way, by ensuring that all staff contribute and feel a sense of ownership of the changes made. Choosing the remodelling change process is the single most important step that organizations make in addressing their challenges and embarking on the journey of change.

As a result of its success in helping schools implement the National Agreement, the DfES asked the NRT to adapt the remodelling change process to help manage a range of other major changes in the public sector, including the implementation of extended services in and around schools, performance management and targeted youth support.

This new, broader and integrated role for the NRT resulted in its full assimilation into the Training and Development Agency for Schools (TDA) in April 2006 (see Figure 3.1). This process began when the NRT merged with the TTA in September 2005.

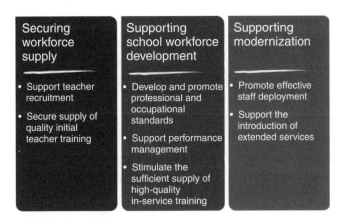

Securing workforce supply

- Support teacher recruitment
- Secure supply of quality initial teacher training

Supporting school workforce development

- Develop and promote professional and occupational standards
- Support performance management
- Stimulate the sufficient supply of high-quality in-service training

Supporting modernization

- Promote effective staff deployment
- Support the introduction of extended services

Figure 3.1 The role of the TDA (TDA, 2007).

In addition to its work with teachers, the TTA was given a new remit that included the training and continuing professional development of the expanding wider workforce in schools, with a broader role in the government's plans to improve services for children, young people and families.

The TDA's responsibility for workforce reform is outlined in Strategic Aim 4 of its Corporate Plan of 2005/2008 (TDA, 2005b, page 10), which states:

> We will use the lessons learned from the NRT project to identify priorities for our future work on supporting schools through the next stages of workforce and work practice reform before we take full responsibility for remodelling in 2006.

Extended services in and around schools

In 2005, before the TDA was formed, the NRT was asked by the DfES to apply its remodelling change process to an 'extended services in and around schools' one-year pilot.

The pilot was designed to help schools meet the requirements of the Every Child Matters agenda – a new approach to the wellbeing of children and young people from birth to age 19. The government's aim is for every child, whatever their background or their circumstances, to have the support they need to:

- be healthy
- stay safe
- enjoy and achieve
- make a positive contribution
- achieve economic wellbeing.

This means that all organizations involved with providing services to children – from schools, to hospitals, to police, to youth services and voluntary groups – are teaming up in new ways, sharing information and working together, to protect children and young people from harm and help them achieve their full potential in life.

From the beginning, the NRT aimed to ensure that local authorities and schools understood the links between Every Child Matters, extended services and multi-agency working (see the Figure 3.2).

The extended services in and around schools pilot involved the NRT – and the remodelling change process – in supporting local authorities and helping the pilot schools develop the extended schools' core offer. Schools were well placed to get involved in this work as they had increased their capacity, flexibility and capability by working through the remodelling change process to implement the requirements of the National Agreement.

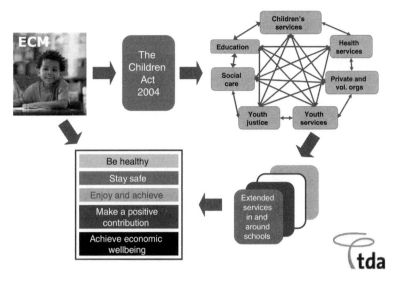

Figure 3.2 Providing extended services in and around schools is vital to delivering the five Every Child Matters outcomes (TDA, 2007).

The extended schools core offer states that by 2010, where there is local demand, all schools should offer access to:

- High-quality childcare provided on the school site or through other local providers, with supervised transport arrangements where appropriate, available 8.00am to 6.00pm all year round.
- A varied programme of activities such as homework clubs and study support, sport, music tuition, dance and drama, arts and crafts, special interest clubs such as chess and first aid courses, visits to museums and galleries, learning a foreign language, volunteering, business and enterprise activities.
- Parenting support, including information sessions for parents at key transition points, parenting programmes run with the support of other children's services, and family learning sessions to allow children to learn with their parents.
- Swift and easy access to a wide range of specialist support services (delivered on school sites where possible), such as speech therapy, child and adolescent mental health services (CAMHS), family support services, intensive behaviour support, and sexual health services.
- Wider community access to school facilities including ICT, sports and arts facilities and adult learning.

The remodelling change process proved itself a very adept and powerful tool in helping schools develop appropriate and sustainable extended services.

The independent National Foundation for Educational Research (NFER) evaluation of remodelling in 2006 reports that initial pilot schools were positive about the support provided by the NRT for the extended schools programme. Local authorities and schools that were involved recognized that they were at an early stage of developing extended services, but felt that they were making good progress and that extended services had made a positive contribution to meeting the needs of their local communities.

The evaluation concludes by stating that the work of the NRT is:

> . . . having a positive impact on local authorities, schools, children and young people and local communities. (Easton *et al.*, 2006)

The extended services in and around schools agenda moved into a national roll-out in 2005 and, by March 2008, more than 10,000 schools across England were providing the full core extended schools offer:

> As we set about developing extended services we went through a workforce remodelling process and the decision we took was that teachers should be free to teach, and that we should use a range of other professionals and support staff to make this possible. (Chris Abbott, headteacher of South Hunsley secondary school)

Benefits

Working through the remodelling change process has led to more and more schools seizing the opportunity to collaborate in order to provide joined-up local extended services. This collaboration is not only with other schools, but also with other organizations, individuals and agencies, enabling schools to tap into the richness of resources that exist in their local communities.

For example, many schools are working more collaboratively with local social and health services, the police, voluntary organizations and parents. Secondary schools, particularly those with 16 to 19 year olds, are also working more closely with the further education sector and other local providers for this age group.

The impact and benefits of partnership working are many – not least a whole range of extended services for children and young people.

Remodelling case study: Gateshead Local Authority

Gateshead is one of three local authorities that recently took part in a Swift and Easy Access (SEA) remodelling pathfinder, facilitated by the TDA. The pathfinder ran between January and July 2007. At the local level it involved the local authority, children's trust partners, voluntary sector organizations and schools.

- A major and early benefit of the pathfinder has been the development of close collaborative working between the extended schools team, the Raising Achievement Service and the Children's Centres.
- The initial work of the change teams was encouraging and supported the involved schools to work more closely with the range of agencies and other organizations (not always the obvious ones) that help support children and young people in the pathfinder area, for example, health and housing. A steering group now oversees the practical implementation of the model, identifying gaps and duplication in existing service provision.

A recent (2007) PricewaterhouseCoopers' report *Independent Study into School Leadership* reported that remodelling and the development of extended services are delivering a range of benefits, not least a very positive shift in school culture. For example, the study reports that:

- The raison d'être of schools is different now, and they are working to a new agenda.
- In particular, there is a new juxtaposition of learning and social agendas.
- The school workforce looks different . . . and is broader.
- Schools are really committed to listening and responding to what their communities need. (page 156)

The study also reports that school leadership is now more shared – schools are led more by teams, not individuals. Leadership teams also look very different than in the past, not least as many of the people in them are not teachers. The study adds that strong leaders or managers in other sectors might have a valuable role to play in schools of the future. It also states that all of the changes will be beneficial for pupils, schools, parents and society as a whole.

More details of these changes and benefits, and many other benefits of the new ways that schools are now working, are described in the broad range of extended schools case studies on the TDA website: www.tda.gov.uk/remodelling.aspx (TDA, 2008b).

School improvement planning

The development of extended services, and the associated remodelling work, needs to be included in school improvement plans. While many schools have always been very organized and professional in their planning, others have not been quite as well-ordered.

To make the most of remodelling – and so achieve the Every Child Matters outcomes, develop extended services and raise standards in the long term – this needed to be addressed.

The TDA's answer was to adapt the remodelling change process to address school improvement planning. The result is a modular and very flexible school improvement planning 'framework' – comprising activities and tools based firmly on remodelling principles. For example:

- The framework's tools and activities are accessible, adaptable (schools can tailor them to their own circumstances) and can be easily built into existing school improvement activities.
- The tools and activities make it possible to engage staff, parents, pupils and the wider community in planning a meaningful way from the outset.
- The framework enables schools to monitor and measure the impact of their planning activities on pupils.

> I looked at the package and thought: I've had 97 people this week who've told me they could improve my self-evaluation form, they could improve my improvement plan, they can develop my school, and they never do . . . they don't do what they say they will. The difference with this was it really has done exactly what we wanted. (Diana Hewitson, headteacher, Kells Lane Primary School, TDA, 2007)

> I think the beauty of this toolkit is that it actually cuts down on the work because it helps you have a more focused consultation. As part of the consultation we had present many members of our multi-agency community, for example educational welfare officers, the youth offending team, people from CAMHS mental health service and we've noticed that, as a result of having person-to-person communication with these agencies and people, we've seen an increase in the number of successful referrals we've been able to make. (Smita Bora, vice principal, Westminster Academy, TDA, 2007)

The framework emphasizes the needs of the whole child and enables schools to deliver and demonstrate improved standards and achievement by putting the child at the centre of school planning. Its primary objective is to help schools evaluate, plan and design the total learning environment, within the school improvement planning cycle, by explicitly linking the Every Child Matters (ECM) outcomes with standards in order to raise pupil attainment.

The framework was tested, developed and honed during a one-year pilot, involving 150 schools. Further detail on the School Improvement Planning framework can be found at www.tda.gov.uk/schoolimprovement

Remodelling in practice

The case study below, which is a composite of the work of a number of real remodelling schools (and includes examples of work around implementing the national agreement as well as extended services), helps bring many of the activities and benefits outlined in the online TDA case studies into a single story.

Leiston consortium

Leiston consortium includes a secondary school, four primary schools, an infant school, a junior school, a special school, a children's centre based at one of the primary schools and a pupil referral unit. Other than two rural primaries, all of the schools are situated on the outskirts of a large metropolitan area.

The schools originally came together as part of an Excellence in Cities' Education Action Zone and have continued as a consortium as part of the local extended services offer. Each school retains its own governing body. There is a consortium steering group made up of governors and headteachers from each of the schools and the heads of the children's centre and the pupil referral unit. The extended schools coordinator, who is based at the secondary school, is an adviser to the steering group.

The secondary is a foundation school and the others are community schools. The steering group receives funding from each school (based on pupil numbers) and from income generated through the charity it runs. The steering group also runs a trading company. All profits from the trading company are fed back into the charity, which has two key aims – to improve opportunities for all pupils within the consortium and to improve opportunities for communities serviced by the schools within the consortium.

The trading company earns its money from running childcare and community lettings. Monies generated from providing services to other schools outside the consortium and from pupil conferences help the schools find their share of the extended schools funding.

The consortium serves a relatively disadvantaged area and this is reflected by a 38 per cent free school meals entitlement across the consortium as a whole. The area served by the consortium also has more advantageous areas, and one of the most notable changes in the last five years is the rising number of children from middle-class backgrounds now attending many of the schools.

Reasons for this include the very positive Ofsted reports, that the schools now regularly get, dramatically improving results at Key Stages 2, 3 and 4, and the massive changes taking place in the post-16 curriculum at Leithwood Maths and Science College, which has managed to increase its post-16 numbers from 140 to 300 in just five years.

In 2003, the consortium schools realized that they needed to buy into the extended schools agenda despite the fact that the agenda had not yet been spelled out. None of the schools in the consortium were involved in the full service extended schools agenda, but all had integrated the values that underpin the Every Child Matters agenda within their schools' ethos. At this stage, the pupil referral unit was not part of the consortium – it joined in 2005 – and the Children's Centre had not been built. It opened in 2005 on the Aston Community Primary School site, the largest of the primary schools in the consortium, with 450 pupils.

The schools involved adapted quickly to the remodelling process in order to implement the national agreement. While neither the secondary nor the special schools faced many difficulties, all of the primary schools found the remodelling change process challenging, particularly with the emotional change required as they adopted a more inclusive approach to team working with support staff.

The idea that experienced teaching assistants and instructors were capable of leading lessons without a teacher always being present was the cause of some resistance in the schools, before it became accepted through seeing it work very well in practice.

There was also a number of quick wins. For example, in Aston Community Primary School the school change team recommended the three most experienced teaching assistants train as higher level teaching assistants. As two of them already had GCSE A* to C grade equivalents in literacy and numeracy, and were very experienced, they rapidly qualified through the assessment-only route.

Another area of resistance to change came in 2005, when the Year 6 teachers were told they could no longer invigilate their pupils during the Key Stage 2 National Curriculum tests. Some of the teachers felt this was a dereliction of duty and they were convinced results would suffer, but the change teams in each school had collaboratively prepared for this change and the headteachers had facilitated the necessary alterations.

Results did go down in one school, but this was mostly due to three children being absent from the maths exam (the school was a one-form entry school with 28 pupils in Year 6). Results improved in all the other schools, and at Aston they improved dramatically.

In all schools there have been further improvements in 2007. The A Level results improved at Leithwood for the third year in a row in 2007, but what pleased the headteacher even more was a 10 percentage point rise in the five or more GCSE A*s to Cs and a big improvement in the maths results.

There were some initial problems at Leithwood Maths and Science College when PPA was introduced for all teachers in 2005. The school, which runs on a 60-period fortnight, already timetabled eight periods a fortnight for all teachers for non-contact time for the purposes of PPA – but this time, for many years, had been flexible. Any of the eight periods (or any non-contact period) could be used for cover, although according to the cover policy no teacher should cover more than once a fortnight over the period of a term. This was clearly stated in the cover policy and was adhered to, with evidence reported to the three teacher unions (NUT, NASUWT and ATL) in the school at the end of each term.

The deputy headteacher in charge of the curriculum proposed the above practice should continue and teaching staff and the unions agreed. While she liked this option, the headteacher was concerned about its veracity so she invited the school change team to check with the NRT. The NRT suggested this option was not acceptable, and that at least for teachers teaching between 51 and 54 periods a fortnight, six periods needed to be timetabled as PPA, in the same way as a subject. For teachers teaching between 41 and 50 periods, at least five periods needed to be designated in the same way and so on.

This caused a real challenge in the school in the summer term of 2005 as timetables were being written, but, having been given the go-ahead from the NRT, the change team felt more confident in insisting on this approach, despite arguments that the current policy was reasonably generous. The change team dug in, and reasonably quickly the unions began to see the potential gains. The headteacher was not opposed to this and convinced the governing body that more money needed to be spent on supply provision.

The deputy headteacher was furious and still blames the local workforce agreement monitoring group, the NRT and the school change team for his 'forced' resignation. However, the school has now appointed a deputy headteacher more in tune with the national agreement and totally committed to extended services. He has already organized a 2007 summer programme, attended by over 450 pupils at the school and, with the school's feeder primaries (including some not in the consortium), he has developed a transition programme from KS2 to KS3.

The consortium now includes a social worker, a school nurse and a policewoman. They are based on the secondary school site, but regularly visit the other schools in the consortium. These three workers, although not employed by the schools, are accepted as members of staff by other staff members and pupils of all the schools. Despite early suspicion, the policewoman now faces a lot less antagonism from the young people at the pupil referral unit – particularly since she started coaching the football team, which has enjoyed some success in the local schools' league.

A further advantage of having these three workers based on-site is that they are able to use their networks to help with swift and easy access to support services when necessary. Although they haven't done so yet, the consortium is planning to employ two parent support advisers, starting in the new academic year.

All of the schools now have a pupil council and each year pupils run two conferences: one primary and one secondary. The secondary pupils help the primary pupils run their conference and Year 5 and Year 6 pupils from the primary sector are invited to the secondary conference. Both conferences are also attended by schools outside the consortium.

The secondary pupils were thrilled this year when a school from France and a school from Scotland sent delegates. They hope next year to raise enough money so that a school they link with in Ghana will be able to send delegates. Both conferences have attracted wide interest with the result that it has become easier to attract keynote speakers of some repute.

In a recent survey of staff across the consortium, 86 per cent stated they believed they now enjoyed a better work/life balance, 93 per cent suggested that they felt more involved in decision making in their schools and were listened to, and almost 95 per cent said that they felt that collaboration between staff within their schools and between schools was much better than it had been even when they were part of the Education Action Zone. In the same survey, staff also said pupil behaviour had improved remarkably, since pupils had become more involved in the management of their school.

The senior leadership teams in each of the involved schools agree that remodelling, although at times difficult and painful, is helping their schools raise standards and enjoy greater success. Three of the headteachers also stated that it was now easier to attract and engage talented staff.

One headteacher said:

> No matter what job we advertise we now get a surfeit of applications that governors find difficult to shortlist. Several governors have suggested that they should delegate appoint-ment responsibility to me for all but the most senior posts. But it's a role I'm loathe to take on except for main grade teachers and senior support staff. It makes the process quicker, but I think, if it was only me doing the interviewing and choosing, people apply-ing would feel short-changed. To get around this problem I always involve a member of the SLT and the line manager in the interviewing process; sometimes I also include a staff governor.

The headteacher of Leithwood says it was very helpful that the workforce agreement monitoring group agreed to use the TDA to support the introduction of the new regu-lations on performance management. She adds that Leithwood is continuing to use remodelling to review all workforce modernization, including the review of Teaching and Learning Responsibility payments.

She says:

> Remodelling is helping the school build a more professional and personal approach to teaching and learning in the school. Across the whole consortium we are beginning to better understand how to develop a much more personalized approach to learning. I believe that remodelling brings two things that have often been absent in school plan-ning: first, the involvement of a wider range of people – we now include representatives of the student body and parents, where appropriate, in our change teams – and, second, the deeper stage of the change process forces us to think more deeply about the issues, rather than leap to a solution we might later regret. And the remodelling tools are fantastic. Staff now use remodelling tools, such as problem-solving team building, regu-larly and all teachers are encouraged to use 'what went well/even better if' in the last five minutes of their lessons. The upper school staff, particularly teachers in the sixth

form, are really pleased that we are using remodelling to introduce a new 14 to 19 curriculum and we already have other secondary schools and the local further education (FE) college working together on the diplomas.

The deputy headteacher of Croftlander Primary School, a school of 360 pupils, is equally excited about the modernization agenda. She is particularly excited about the school's involvement in the School Improvement Plan pilot, run by the TDA. She admits she originally found it incredibly daunting and felt like a failure. When pressed she admits to crying in the evenings in front of her husband, during the original start to the programme. But she now says that this programme is more exciting than anything she has ever done before. She says:

It brings together all those initiatives the government keeps throwing out. We've suddenly found a way to join them up. Actually, I'm beginning to believe that by joining them up in this way they aren't a string of different initiatives but all the same thing driving the same way. The agenda becomes obvious once you use this approach. Why didn't we see it before?

Pupils are also benefiting from the changes. Parmjeet, Year 6, says:

When I learned who my teacher was in Year 5 I was really scared. It was the same teacher I'd had in Year 1 and he had really scared me. I hated coming to school. He never seemed to smile and, although he wasn't cruel, he didn't seem to want to join in with us. Now he's changed. Maybe he prefers teaching older kids, I don't know. But he's much more relaxed with us and laughs and jokes a lot. He's always smiling. And we celebrate things more. My most exciting experience was when I was put in charge of the India project. I explained that I was born in England and knew little about India but he said that didn't matter and now was a good time to learn – and I could help the rest of the class, including him. When I asked him how I would get the information necessary, he told me to talk to my parents and, if necessary, use the internet to fill in the detail. My brother has a computer at home which he let me use. I found out that my grandfather was a friend of Satyajit Ray when he was boy. I have to admit that I didn't understand the significance of that story but my teacher was really excited by it.

Louise, Year 5, is more reticent, but she thinks the school is now more open and she is a lot happier than she was in Year 2. She says bullying by older pupils had been a real problem, and the lack of teacher interest if bullying was reported had also been a problem. She says:

But everything is different now. There is bullying but as soon as any of us complain someone somewhere follows it up. In my early years I hated school. Now I really enjoy it.

I hope to go to Leithwood. I know that is a really hard school to get into, but I'm going to try my hardest.

Targeted youth support

The success of remodelling in schools led to the DfES, in 2005, asking the NRT to deploy remodelling in the much wider, and even more challenging and complex public service environment, of reforming targeted support for vulnerable young people across England.

The NRT was asked to adapt the school remodelling change process and run a one-year pathfinder in 14 children's trusts around the country. This adapted process is the example of the remodelling process featured most prominently in the next chapter.

The government's *Youth Matters Green Paper* (DfES, 2005) set out a vision of integrated youth support services. The aim is to help all young people achieve the five Every Child Matters' outcomes through the coherent, young person-centred delivery of information, advice and guidance, support, development opportunities and positive activities.

Reformed targeted youth support brings this vision to life for vulnerable teenagers who are likely to need help and opportunities from a range of different agencies and who have the most to gain from a timely, coordinated and effective response.

Getting this right gives vulnerable young people the chance to enjoy their teenage years, build positive futures and avoid a range of potential serious problems. Target outcomes include improved attainment and the reduction of: persistent pupil absence; substance misuse; youth offending; under-18 conceptions; and the percentage of 16–18 year olds who are not in education, employment or training.

This reform of targeted youth support builds on changes already under way in young people's services by drawing them together into a coherent whole designed for, and largely shaped by, vulnerable young people and their families and carers. At its core, it aims to ensure the needs of vulnerable teenagers are identified early and met by agencies working together effectively.

The targeted youth support pathfinders started working through the remodelling change process in early 2006. The process gave the pathfinders the method and tools they needed to redesign targeted youth support services and delivery models in order to improve outcomes for vulnerable young people.

This was a hugely complex task as the change process needed to encompass – and bring together into multi-agency teams – a vast range of different organizations supporting young people, including: local authorities, children's centres, health services, social services, voluntary and community sector agencies, Connexions, education welfare, behaviour support, drugs and alcohol services, schools, sexual health services, teenage parent support workers, special educational needs coordinators, CAMHS, counselling services, information advice and guidance providers, housing and housing support, youth offending services, the police – and so on!

Results

The pathfinder was very challenging. It was also a great success. The remodelling change process delivered many benefits. For example, it gave children's trusts a practical tool with which to deliver the Youth Matters and Every Child Matters agendas by:

- Keeping a focus throughout on service users and improving outcomes.
- Being inclusive – valuing the input of staff and stakeholders, young people, parents and communities in creating and implementing plans for tailored change in an atmosphere of consensus.
- Identifying where change is necessary – helping children's trusts uncover and analyse the needs of young people and their families and identify strengths and weaknesses in service provision.
- Providing a flexible step-by-step framework – wherever you are in delivering this agenda for young people, the toolkit can help.
- Building upon existing good practice and children's trust planning.
- Taking account of the emotional, political and rational factors of change.
- Ensuring equal opportunity for all during the implementation process.
- Helping develop and deliver sustainable improvement.

Targeted youth support case study: Leicester City

One of our key challenges has been identifying stakeholders in our scope area. It's incredible how many people support young people in the area – even now, more are coming out of the woodwork. We thought we knew who was active in the area but we didn't know the half of it. Mapping out provision has been much more complex and time-consuming than we expected.

An associated challenge is working out what's needed to get these people onboard the targeted youth support remodelling project. For two months I felt like a glorified administrator, calling people and asking standard questions about what they do. Perhaps our information department should already have had this information. The targeted youth support project is really highlighting these sorts of issues. (Rita Chohan, project coordinator, targeted youth support pathfinder – Leicester City, ECM case study, 2006)

The change process proved itself a very effective way of linking all the many initiatives that impact on young people and of ensuring that young people, their parents and their communities are fully engaged in the development of targeted youth support.

The process also created a real momentum and enthusiasm among stakeholders and helped link, enhance and accelerate existing good practice, encourage multi-agency collaboration and service integration, and ultimately improve service delivery – tailored to each local area – and outcomes for young people.

In short, the remodelling change process enabled the pathfinders to develop sustainable and effective delivery models that are owned collectively and delivered collaboratively.

> The pathfinder has shifted the targeted youth support agenda to centre stage in the authority. It has properly aligned it within *Every Child Matters* and other policy areas, and has shown the power to influence strategic thinking. It has joined up all of the main agencies and will have a major impact in Leicester City. (Paul Vaughan, head of youth services and targeted youth support pathfinder sponsor, Leicester City)

The targeted youth support framework

The targeted youth support remodelling change process was developed and honed during the one-year pathfinder into a highly practical and precisely fit-for-purpose remodelling framework – comparable, but necessarily more complex than the school improvement framework.

This targeted youth support remodelling framework, which is firmly based on learning from the pathfinder and on the remodelling change process, is currently being used to successfully facilitate the roll-out of targeted youth support reform to local areas across the whole of England.

The targeted youth support roll-out is now the responsibility of the Youth Support Team at the DCSF. The TDA project team remains involved to advise and help ensure success.

The outcomes of the pilot project, including details of the tailored pilot remodelling process, can be found on the Every Child Matters website: www.everychildmatters.gov.uk

Generic process

The next chapter explores the practical mechanics of the generic remodelling change process and its five clear stages in depth. The targeted youth support pathfinder process – and its associated key tasks, activities and tools – is used as the main illustrative example.

4 Remodelling: the process

As the previous chapter described, the remodelling change process is underpinned by academic rigour and a wealth of practical experience and learning – that is, it has been shown, again and again, to work. It is this rigour and its highly successful track record that gives remodelling a very solid claim to be the best of the best.

The remodelling change process enables individuals and organizations to collaboratively address issues and come up with made-to-measure solutions – one size does not fit all – and produce sustainable plans, actions and outcomes.

It is important, though, not to think of remodelling as a finished product. Rather, it is a dynamic and ever-developing cycle of continuous improvement that can be easily and powerfully adapted and tailored to address any individual change situation – large or small, simple or complex, public or private sector. This inherent adaptability ensures remodelling remains relevant, powerful and sustainable. It is its greatest strength.

Each of the five distinct stages of the TDA remodelling change process – mobilize, discover, deepen, develop and deliver – involves a number of key tasks and activities. These five stages are discussed in depth later on in this chapter.

If any of the remodelling tasks or activities are not relevant to a particular change situation, or if they have been carried out already by the involved organizations, they are either not included in the tailored remodelling process or they are incorporated and built on within the process (without the work needing to be carried out again).

The remodelling change process, together with a range of business tools and skilled facilitation, can be applied to any context and any organization, or group of organizations, to enable them to lead, manage and sustain change.

Tailoring the process to each change situation is a highly skilled job – one that should be carried out by facilitators or consultants with a deep understanding of remodelling. In some instances the core process may hardly need to change at all, in others it may need to change a great deal. For example, the targeted youth support change process, in response to learning from the pathfinder, has developed into a change framework even more exactly tailored to the complexities of the agenda.

The change process is tried and tested and we trust it. It is a very powerful mechanism and what it has delivered for us would have cost a fortune through other means. This will definitely remain as core business for our change for children programme. I wish I wasn't retiring and could stay with it. (Ron Skilling, Assistant Director, Children's Services, Knowsley)

Tools

The effectiveness of the remodelling change process is further enhanced by the use of a wide range of business tools. These tools, which are not exclusive to remodelling, have a particularly powerful impact in the remodelling change process as their use is specifically tailored to each change situation to ensure that they are used at the right time in the right way in order to add maximum value.

The business tools that are often employed during the remodelling change process include: the five whys; brown paper planning; brainstorming; week/day in the life of; problem solving, team building; the prioritization matrix; managing uncertainty; stakeholder mapping; project management templates – roles and responsibilities; what's working/what's so-so/what's not working; get to know you and sentence build icebreakers; fishbone analysis; force-field analysis; and journey-mapping.

These tools, and others used in the remodelling process, come from many sources. Some of them will already be known to many organizations. In-depth details of the tools listed above can be found at www.tda.gov.uk/remodelling/managingchange/tools.aspx

Several of these tools are explained in a different context with background reading in Suzanne Turner's book, *Tools for Success* (2002).

Facilitation

To be fully effective, the remodelling process needs to be tailored to each individual change situation. As mentioned above, it is hard, if not impossible, to successfully do this without the advice and support of external remodelling facilitators with detailed experience of this work.

In addition, the tasks, activities and tools at each stage of the change process are often given extra muscle and direction through the expertise of these external facilitators. Facilitator support can be light or heavy, depending on what is required and the complexity of the change situation.

It is also important that organizations working through the remodelling change process have their own skilled facilitators, as many of the activities and tasks of the process require strong facilitation. Ultimately, the remodelling change process is a highly inclusive process, run by a cross-section of staff within organizations and tailored and targeted towards organizations' individual requirements and aims.

Change curve

The expertise and support of external facilitators is particularly critical during the more challenging early periods of the remodelling change process, when individuals and organizations typically experience quite a dip in their confidence, enthusiasm and motivation for change.

This emotional dip – which is a consequence of rational, political and emotional factors – typically occurs shortly after the beginning of the change process when the range and implication of the changes that need to be made become fully apparent. The dip bottoms out and moves into a more positive and enthused stage, but it can continue until solutions start to be developed.

This change curve is not exclusive to the remodelling process. It is an explanation of human reaction during any change, be it personal, professional or any other aspect of life. However, linking the remodelling process with the change curve makes it easier to identify periods when people may be at their lowest and when support is most required. It should not be assumed that every person will be affected in exactly the same way or at exactly the same time. What can be predicted, though, is that everyone will go through the same emotional process (see Figure 4.1).

Without expert support to help them understand the emotional dip and, rather than be daunted by it, appreciate it as a creative part of their change process, organizations can lose heart and compromise their ambitions – at best snatching at instant solutions that have little if no relevance to their core issues and requirements and so are doomed to disappoint.

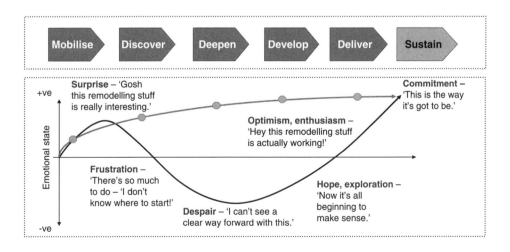

Figure 4.1 Remodelling and the emotional curve (TDA, 2007).

The support of external facilitators during this critical time helps individuals and organizations lead change and develop tailored solutions that enable them to succeed, and continue to succeed, into the long term.

In *Leading Change* (1996), Harvard Business School professor John Kotter identifies eight reasons, or issues, that explain why change agendas often fail. The remodelling process is designed to address each of these issues and ensure they are overcome.

1. *Allowing too much complacency to set in*: leaders often fail to create a real sense of urgency among their staff. A sense of urgency drives change.
2. *Failing to create teams with enough power to lead the change*: too often teams created to lead change either lack the necessary influence or fail to work together as a team. True transformation requires teams that are fully committed to leading change.
3. *Underestimating the power of vision*: vision plays a crucial role in providing the inspiration, direction, alignment and the cohesion necessary to ensure that enough staff are involved to take the necessary action to ensure change.
4. *Under-communicating or failing to communicate the vision successfully*: too often teams leading change fail to communicate effectively to those who need to implement the change.
5. *Allowing obstacles, real or imagined, to block the vision*: sometimes blockages are imagined and it becomes necessary to convince people that change can take place and will improve the situation. At other times blockages are real; for example, the organizational structure is wrong or a senior manager is obstructing change.
6. *Failing to create short-term gains*: major changes can take a long time to embed. There need to be some short-term gains to ensure that those experiencing change remain motivated.
7. *Declaring victory too soon*: too often organizations think they have succeeded at the first real sign of improvement. This leads to a reduced sense of urgency and the change process can slow considerably or stop altogether.
8. *Neglecting to embed the changes in the culture*: change endures only when it becomes part of the ethos and culture of an organization. New practices, attitudes and behaviours are lost quickly unless people are aware of, and can identify, what is making the difference.

(Adapted from Kotter, 1996)

The five stages of the change process

The tasks, tools and activities that support each remodelling stage can be used in a stand-alone way when appropriate, but the remodelling change process is far more powerful when followed sequentially in its entirety. Most organizations have experience and skills they can use in addition to the tasks, activities and tools provided in the process. This is encouraged.

While the exact tasks, tools and activities carried out during the five stages of the remodelling change process depend on the individual change situation and the organization or organizations involved, a number of core activities are commonly carried out during each stage. These activities ensure the achievements of each stage are accomplished before moving onto the next stage.

The activities listed as examples in the mobilize, discover, deepen, develop and deliver (NB to ensure consistency in this book, I will use these TDA-owned names for the remodelling stages). The sections below come from a version of the remodelling change process specifically adapted to help local authority partners reform their targeted youth support. Much of the information below is featured online at www.everychildmatters. gov.uk/deliveringservices/targetedyouthsupport/

As mentioned in the previous chapter, targeted youth support reforms build on changes already under way in young people's services in England by drawing them together into a coherent whole designed for, and largely shaped by, vulnerable young people and their families and carers.

There is always, and inevitably, a temptation for organizations to look for solutions quickly without working through all of the remodelling change process. This is a natural behaviour but it should be avoided at all costs. A great many of the organizations that have worked through the remodelling change process have reported instances when the process revealed their assumptions were not comprehensive or accurate. Accuracy is vital if effective solutions tailored to meet specific needs are to be developed.

> Before the pathfinder we had initiatives to redesign our targeted youth services, but without the structure that the targeted youth support remodelling change process has brought us they stalled and we lost momentum. (Bridget Cooper, head of youth service and targeted youth support pathfinder manager, Worcestershire)

While there is no set timescale for the initial run-through of the remodelling change process, it is typically run over a period of six months to a year. Once the process is established, most organizations chose to continue to run it into the long term to resolve new issues and challenges as they appear.

Mobilize

The first – mobilize – stage of the remodelling process is where all those involved in leading change (which may be managers and other staff from one organization, or managers, staff and other stakeholders from a collaboration of a number of organizations) commit to the remodelling change process and build their awareness of the changes required to improve their performance and outcomes.

> The targeted youth support remodelling change process has fully involved stakeholders and built a belief and engagement – this is key to better multi-agency working. (Anthony May, assistant director young peoples' division and targeted youth support pathfinder sponsor, Nottinghamshire)

The target outcomes they are aiming for can be more or less anything, but existing examples include improved business productivity and efficiency, improved teaching and learning in schools, and improved outcomes for vulnerable young people in local areas.

The mobilize stage of the remodelling change process affirms the top priority or priorities of organizations and recognizes the importance of all stakeholders. This is the beginning of the move to a culture that encourages closer collaboration between all those involved in change.

During the mobilize stage, it is important to understand what the key stakeholders believe are the major issues facing the organization(s). Their views should be reflected in the scope of the change project plans, to ensure that these plans fit within the organization's strategic agenda and are fully aligned with its priorities for reform.

A key task during this stage is choosing and appointing the right project sponsor and project manager. Sponsors and managers should be well networked and, above all, have credibility in the organization(s) and be able to influence and convince others. Their personality, skills and aptitude are far more important than the department (or organization, etc.) they are from. Their roles are vital to the success of the remodelling change process.

During the mobilize stage, individuals and organizations are at the beginning, or top, of the change curve – motivated and aware of the need for positive change, but not yet fully aware of the minutiae and depth of change that needs to take place.

At the end of the mobilize stage, organizations should understand in-depth what their change agenda is and the potential level of change required. Senior managers need to be committed to this change and a remodelling project team (in schools, this will be a school change team – change teams are discussed in more depth later in this chapter and in Chapter 5) should be in place with the skills and capacity to manage the change process.

In addition to the above achievements, a realistic and clear needs-based scope for the remodelling project should be in place and all stakeholders should be identified and effective communications processes arranged. Strong governance and reporting mechanisms also need to be created and a robust project plan developed.

As mentioned previously, while the exact activities carried out during the mobilize stage (and during the other four stages of the change process) depend on the individual change situation and the organization(s), involved, a number of core activities are commonly carried out during this stage.

These activities ensure the achievements for mobilize mentioned above are accomplished before moving onto the next stage of the change process. In the targeted youth support version of the remodelling change process these activities include:

• Choosing the project manager, project sponsor and senior management group. The project manager, project sponsor and senior management group drive and shape the remodelling change process and are the cornerstone of successful and directed change. It is therefore very important to choose the right people.

- A launch presentation to the senior management group. This presentation clarifies the aims and objectives of change agenda and gains agreement for the project process and timescale.
- Undertaking training. The project manager and project sponsor should undertake basic training for their new roles.
- Stakeholder mapping and engagement. This enables the project team to manage stakeholders at the outset and throughout the project. It helps identify work that needs to be done with individuals and teams and ensure alignment around project objectives.
- A planning workshop. This engages key stakeholders in shaping potential changes.
- Creating a project initiation document. This document captures all project objectives and plans at the outset, so progress can be steered and measured. It records the purpose, scope, process, roles, responsibilities and timescales of the project and is signed off by the project sponsor.
- A communications plan. This is part of the project initiation document and an ongoing key activity to keep stakeholders informed and involved throughout the change process. The communications plan identifies key stakeholders to communicate with and sets out ways to do this.

Discover

During this stage, senior managers, operational staff and other stakeholders uncover the detail of the current state of their organization(s). To ensure this detail is understood in as broad a context as possible, the views of senior staff should be balanced with the views of front-line staff and all other stakeholders – including external customers.

> The change process has hugely increased the engagement of the workforce in the agenda. In the past, discussions around this would be in silos. As a result of the process they are now integrated. (Alan Dinning, Deputy Director Integrated Children's Services, Hertfordshire)

Any existing and relevant work carried out by organizations should, of course, be included in this stage. For example, to identify the knowledge they already have and any gaps in that knowledge, public organizations such as local authorities may need to re-examine existing needs assessments, service provision information, public service agreement measures, joint area reviews, annual performance assessment recommendations and survey results that they have already created.

This re-examination helps organizations avoid replicating what has already been done, i.e., time wasting, and helps them build on solid existing data. Existing sources of data, unless fully comprehensive, should be tested and supplemented by additional data uncovered during this discover stage of the remodelling change process.

A key strength of the remodelling change process is that it generates an extensive buy-in from all stakeholder groups at all levels. So any existing sources of data should be recent and gathered alongside material from all staff (from senior managers to front-line staff) so they know their views have been fully heard and will be acted upon. The data taken from selected customers also need to be fully representative of all customer groups.

During the discover stage, organizations often identify potential quick wins – straight-forward and effective changes that can be implemented immediately. Quick wins help build momentum and commitment to the remodelling change process because stakeholders can see it is having an impact on their work and on outcomes. As quick wins are often implemented before the root causes of problems are uncovered during the deepen stage, they can require adjustment in the long term.

At this stage in the change process, it may emerge that challenges are greater than they first appeared. It is normal and expected for individuals and organizations to feel daunted by this. This is the start of the downward part of the change curve. This feeling often continues into the next stage of the process.

At the end of the discover stage the change process project team will be well into assembling a body of evidence that gives a research-based description of the current situation. There will also be an increased awareness of the potential priorities and target benefits of the change process for senior managers and operational and front-line staff.

In addition to these achievements, the remodelling project team and key stakeholders should know and understand the views of senior managers, front-line workers and others involved in change. Data and opinions from these groups should have been collected in many different ways and representatives of all these groups should also be actively contributing to the change process.

All participants in the change process should have broadened their understanding of what is and is not working well by the end of the discover stage, and the remodelling project team should have a greater awareness of how other related organizational changes and initiatives tie into the potential changes they are making.

A number of core activities is commonly carried out during this stage to ensure the achievements for the discover stage, mentioned above, are accomplished before moving on to the next stage of the change process. In the targeted youth support remodelling change process these activities include:

- Developing a first edit of the presentation to the senior management group. This first edit provides an early view of the presentation required at the end of the next – deepen – stage of the process. It provides focus for the data collection and analysis needed over the discover and deepen stages of the process, and identifies any gaps in the data being collected. It is advisable to organize a review of data by colleagues with analytical expertise prior to the presentation, to ensure its rigour.

- Conducting structured interviews that help organizations gather in-depth information from their staff and other stakeholders. This can be a very efficient method of collecting data around the current situation.
- Engaging key customers. Customers' views must be heard and acted upon. Running a workshop for them is one method of establishing their needs and experiences of an organization's service. Customers should be engaged in different ways throughout the change process.
- Holding a collaborative workshop for all stakeholders. This workshop helps different staff groups from an organization or range of organizations understand how their current processes are operating. The workshop can include mapping a customer's service experience of the organization to find out where good practice exists and where there are gaps.

The next stage in the process, Deepen, is where remodelling project teams test findings from the discover stage in greater detail and acquire deeper understanding of the scale of the changes they need to make to achieve their aims.

Deepen

The presentation of the collected and analysed data about the current situation to the organization's or organizations' senior management group takes place at the end of this stage – and the key priority issues to be addressed in the next stage of the change process are decided.

> Addressing vision and leadership enabled the senior group to check that their different services had a shared understanding and vision for the future. They also did some practical work on the skills needed for matrix and multi-agency management. Finally, they thought afresh about the risks that might derail the change process and how to ensure success. They checked the existing action plan against the rational, political and emotional barriers to mobilizing the workforce and against the levers for change they had identified. (Mike Smith, Southwark Local Authority)

During the deepen stage, participants in the change process use the change process and its tools to identify the root causes of the issues uncovered in the discover stage. They establish which issues are causing, or have the potential to cause, the most problems and clarify their impact. To do this successfully, the remodelling project team needs to engage and consult all those involved in the change – including all staff and customer groups.

It is vital to avoid the temptation to jump straight from identifying issues to implementing solutions at this stage. For a solution to be effective, the underlying causes of issues must be identified and understood. This is what the deepen stage is all about.

There is, however, a judgement to be made on how much effort is spent on deepening all issues at this stage. It is important to understand issues in enough detail to be able to decide the priority issues to address, but there is a risk of investigating issues that will not be taken forward as high priorities. It can be better to leave some deepening to the develop stage.

The deepen stage culminates in an in-depth presentation of the current situation to the senior management group. The presentation includes quantitative and qualitative data, an analysis of the root causes of the issues and a series of potential priorities that need addressing if outcomes are to improve.

At the end of this stage, the remodelling project team identifies the separate elements and root causes of the major prioritized issues, and all of those involved in the potential changes will have increased their awareness of potential priorities and target benefits. The quick wins identified during the discover stage may also be implemented at this stage.

In addition to the above achievements, the data collected about the current situation are analysed and presented to the senior management group, and a list of potential priority issues is agreed. The scope established in the project initiation document remains the focus of the project.

It is particularly important to address the emotional and political barriers to change during this stage as well as the rational, straightforward practicalities of change, as it is the time when emotions are typically at the bottom of the change curve, as the scale of the task becomes evident.

A number of core activities is commonly carried out during this stage to ensure the achievements for the deepen stage mentioned above are accomplished before moving on to the next stage of the change process. In the targeted youth support remodelling change process these activities include:

- A generic deepening workshop to help identify the underlying root causes of issues or problems identified during the discover stage.
- Journey-mapping a young person's ('customer's') experience of current services.
- A workshop to help identify the thresholds used by different agencies and services for young people and to understand their implications.
- A risk and resilience workshop to help different agencies and services better understand the risks facing young people and how their resilience to these risks can be increased.
- Developing and delivering the presentation to the senior management group. This is the final version of the presentation, including data and analysis from the discover and deepen stages. The meeting with the senior management group includes agreeing the priorities for the develop and deliver stages of the process.

Develop

The essential purpose of the develop stage of the change process is to develop solutions to the key priority issues. A shared view of the future emerges from this work, as well as the changes needed to get there. Not all solutions are identified, but a vision is established that meets the expectations of the earlier stages of the change process.

> Bringing together practitioners to be part of the solutions has really helped people find the common purpose that we are all working to benefit children and young people. For example, targeted youth support is bringing in the district councils and local voluntary groups in a way that we've never had before. (Bridget Cooper, TYS Project Manager, Worcestershire)

It is this clarity about future provision, underpinned by specific proposals for change based around a series of key priority issues, which is presented to the senior management team and key stakeholders at an implementation meeting at the end of this stage.

Forming a strategy to address the priority issues is part of this meeting. Resources are allocated to areas where they will have the greatest impact. Not every solution progresses beyond this point but those that do have strong senior management commitment.

Addressing the priority issues requires an inclusive and collaborative style of working. To ensure all involved staff and organizations contribute, inclusive change teams are formed around each priority, to work on developing solutions that are realistic, desirable and achievable.

During the develop stage, those involved in the change process are moving up the change curve, well aware of the need for change, enthused and developing solutions.

At the end of the develop stage, one, or a number, of remodelling change teams – consisting of representatives from all relevant stakeholder groups – are operating. These teams have a remit and have received appropriate training. Change teams are key to developing successful solutions.

The change teams work to create a portfolio of solutions for each of the key priority issues that came out of the presentation to senior managers in the previous stage. The teams also develop a plan to deliver these solutions (including the identification of outcome measures) and present it to senior managers and other key stakeholders at the end of this stage.

This meeting ensures strong senior management commitment to the chosen solutions. This includes the allocation of resources for implementation in areas where they will have the greatest impact.

In addition to these achievements, quick wins identified during earlier stages in the change process are in place now, helping create further momentum for change. Further quick wins may also be identified.

A number of core activities are commonly carried out during the develop stage to ensure the achievements mentioned above are accomplished before moving on to the next stage of the change process. In the targeted youth support remodelling change process these activities include:

- The develop stage needs to mobilize change teams from an organization, or range of organizations, to develop solutions to the agreed key priorities. Inclusive change teams help different stakeholders work together effectively to make informed and focused decisions, generate solutions and prioritize and implement sustainable changes. It may also be necessary to mobilize facilitators to help run change team meetings in a structured and effective way.
- A 'fast start' meeting brings everyone together to discuss and form the agenda. This is an efficient and effective way to get change teams with diverse membership to a common point of understanding and begin the task of developing solutions.
- Change teams need to meet regularly to follow the plans developed at the fast start workshop. Teams work together in structured ways to generate a range of possible solutions for presentation at the options development workshop (see below). These solutions are subsequently refined by the change teams into detailed proposals for the presentation of implementation plans to senior managers at the end of this stage.
- An options development workshop is an opportunity for change teams to share their progress with each other, and provide feedback in order to improve the quality of the options they have developed. Change teams should have a clear understanding of what needs to be done in preparation for the presentation of their plans to senior managers by the end of the workshop.
- An evaluation workshop is the last time change teams get together before they present their solutions to senior managers. At this session, change teams evaluate the quality of their solutions and presentations. Participants need to ensure that all proposals integrate into an overall compelling model for the planned changes.
- The change teams present their solutions (including budgets and performance measures), as well as plans for implementing those solutions. The meeting includes collectively agreeing solutions and implementation plans.

The next stage in the remodelling change process, deliver, is where the solutions and plans formed in the develop stage are confirmed and agreed, and where they start to be implemented.

Deliver

During the deliver stage it is essential that a review process is put in place to ensure that solutions are consistent with the key priority issues that came out of presentation to senior managers at the end of the deepen stage of the process – and that they provide the anticipated benefits. Some solutions may need to be modified to ensure all of the changes made contribute to the vision shared by all the participants in the change process.

I struggled at first to see if the whole TYS change process was worthwhile, but I'm glad I went with it because I now know more about what is going on and can verbalize the need for early support and see how it fits with my work with young people in residential care. (Rhona Carr, children in care team residential manager and change team member, South Tyneside)

The review process enables all those involved in the change process to work even more effectively, with each individual (and organization) well supported and confident that his or her work is valued. He or she is able to focus better on core work and reach out more to share his or her experiences, if he or she chooses, with other local and national organizations.

As the remodelling change process ensures that solutions are developed by all stakeholders, there is enthusiasm and commitment around the implementation of these solutions and universal support for their success. The result is that everyone benefits.

During the deliver stage, those involved in the change process are moving quickly up the change curve, implementing solutions that are really making a positive difference to their lives and the performance of their organization(s). Regular monitoring, evaluation and refinement of remodelling solutions are key to their delivery and long-term success.

At the end of the deliver stage a coherent change plan is rolled out, implementation commences, and project goals and benefits start to be achieved. This includes measuring outcomes to assess the impact of the changes.

The activities carried out during the deliver stage to ensure the milestones mentioned above are achieved are very much individual to the organization(s) involved in each remodelling change process. The targeted youth support pathfinders, for example, all developed their own implementation plans tailored to their specific areas. Examples of these plans can be found at http://www.everychildmatters.gov.uk

Sustain

Remodelling has an implicit sixth stage, sustain, as the process encourages and enables positive and lasting change. Remodelling embeds a proactive and collaborative culture where individuals and organizations have the skills, experience, confidence and commitment to apply an effective remodelling approach to all significant challenges at all times into the long term.

Staff become more involved in the running of their organizations, their work/life balance is better and collaboration between staff – and between organizations and other stakeholders – is encouraged and improved.

Individuals and organizations incorporate the additional flexibility, capacity and capability they need into their working lives to meet new challenges and requirements. They develop and incorporate a remodelling cycle of continuous improvement, where

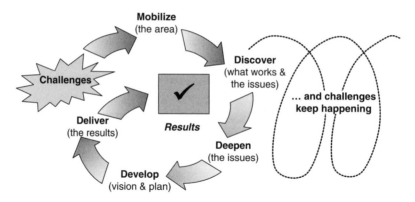

Figure 4.2 The TDA change management process – working into the future (TDA).

performance is assessed and new solutions are created and fed into future plans on an ongoing basis (see Figure 4.2).

A key focus of organizations during this ongoing sustain stage of the change process is on assessing, reviewing and embedding successful changes. This is necessary to keep change dynamic and alive. Organizations also need to focus on:

- *Long-term planning*: plans for ongoing improvements must balance quick wins and longer-term changes. For example, changes need to be phased in order to keep heading towards end goals, while also delivering immediate improvements that impact positively on outcomes.
- *Addressing tensions*: those involved in change need to understand when and where there are tensions between their aims, and develop solutions in a way that retains a focus on successful and shared solutions. This involves communicating the case for change and ensuring the involvement of all staff in decision making.
- *Using evidence to plan changes*: where possible, solutions should draw on evidence from existing successful delivery models and interventions – internal and external.
- *Continuous improvement*: organizations need to develop performance management that ensures a focus on outcomes and reviewing practice on an ongoing basis. New thinking and ways of working need to be checked against quality standards and incorporated into new plans.

The result of embedding a proactive and collaborative remodelling culture is that individuals, organizations and groups of organizations improve standards, attract and engage the best talent, increase their focus and purpose, build professionalism, take the lead in their sector and enjoy greater success.

> The remodelling change process has challenged cultural norms and silos. People often talk a lot about partnership, but don't always deliver it. They talk to each other, but don't

always really work collaboratively. Now they do this and will sit together and challenge their own services and not just other people's. This is a big cultural change and is fundamental to reform. This change process forces them into that position. (Kim Bromley-Derry, former director of Children's Services, South Tyneside – a targeted youth support pathfinder)

5 Remodelling: making it work

For the first time in history our heritage is no longer our destiny. Our dreams are no longer fantasies but possibilities. There isn't a human being who has ever lived who wouldn't want to be alive right now, at this moment so pregnant with promise. Among all your forebears, among all the countless generations who had no hope of progress, among all those whose spirits were betrayed by progress, you are the ones who now stand on the threshold of a new age – the age of revolution. You are blessed beyond belief. Don't falter. Don't hesitate. You were given this opportunity for a reason. Find it. Lead the revolution.

(Hamel, 2002, page 314)

For remodelling to be fully successful there needs to be a shared and compelling reason for change, a clear vision for the future and a coherent plan for getting there. The changes that are planned need to be based on a comprehensive understanding of relevant, often localized, needs and circumstances.

Engaging all key stakeholders – individuals and organizations – at the outset of remodelling in a process that includes building the case for change is therefore essential. Once they are engaged, remodelling goes on to involve these stakeholders in collaboratively addressing issues and problems, and coming up with realistic and sustainable solutions that operate within the context of the organization or group of organizations. This process inevitably provokes rational, political and emotional responses.

A core strength of remodelling is that it is holistically designed to address these human (political and emotional), as well as the more mechanistic (rational), aspects of change. This is why successful remodelling needs to be underpinned by six core remodelling elements (see Figure 5.1):

- shared and effective leadership
- inclusive culture
- constructive collaboration

Figure 5.1 The core elements of remodelling (TDA, 2006).

- proactive and inclusive change team(s)
- proven change process
- rational, political and emotional considerations.

Some of the detail below, and additional information about the core elements of remodelling, can be found online at www.tda.gov.uk/remodelling/managingchange.aspx (TDA, 2006).

Shared and effective leadership

A cornerstone of successful remodelling is open inclusive leadership that provides clear direction and focus, drawing on the contributions of all staff and stakeholders. This facilitative leadership approach constitutes a departure from a more traditional top-down model of command and control.

This departure can initially feel unsettling for those in leadership positions, as it can take some time to work out what their new role looks like and to get used to working in a different and more open way. But, as Albert Einstein suggested, we can't solve problems by using the same kind of thinking we used when we created them.

For lasting change to occur in organizations, the awareness, support and positive contribution of all levels of staff and other relevant stakeholders during the change process is key. The process brings out the inherent creativity within human beings and encourages innovative thinking. Change teams, in particular, as representatives of all staff and stakeholders, need to take a lead role in developing the organizations' vision for change and the route map for getting there. The benefits include:

- staff feel more included and valued;
- much broader and richer insights and ideas for progress;
- staff and stakeholder morale is improved and as result organizational morale and aspiration increase, leading to improved outcomes;
- more people are attracted to apply for jobs and staff want to stay with organizations for the long term;
- shared responsibility, everyone working together and a greater sense of control;
- reduced workload and stress for leaders and staff;
- more honest and direct interactions, including problems being aired and sorted out on the spot;
- a learning culture develops where staff and other stakeholders seek support and challenge while collaborating fully inside and outside the organization.

For example, evidence from schools suggests that remodelling is leading to improved standards of teaching and learning, and improved outcomes for pupils. Remodelling is also leading, and will continue to lead, to improvements in performance in other organizations, both public and private.

A more open, democratic and effective leadership model does not mean the end of a role for the managing director (or equivalent) and the leadership team. Although remodelling involves developing a more open culture, strong core leadership remains a crucial constituent of all successful organizations.

> Remodelling has released the talents of school staff members who have previously been under recognized and has developed leadership skills in many. (Joan Gibson, Oakham Church of England Primary School, Rutland, 2005)

There is a great deal of evidence to support the enduring importance of strong leadership, for example, in the work of leadership gurus such as Peter Senge (1996) and colleagues, John Kotter (1996) and Michael Fullan (2001, 2003), even if the specifics of remodelling are not necessarily part of their agenda.

Leaders need to be seen to be effective role models for all staff in supporting and encouraging positive change. An important aspect of this is delegating responsibility for tackling key challenges to staff with appropriate skills, experience and commitment, irrespective of their position within the organization. The critical importance of leadership is discussed in more detail in Chapter 7.

Inclusive culture

Successful remodelling embeds a positive and ambitious inclusive culture in organizations that enables everyone to play their part in driving a change agenda forward. It is a culture where all staff and stakeholders feel positive and inspired about being part of an organization with a strong, clear, forward-looking and innovative vision; where they are able to fully contribute towards creating opportunities and overcoming key challenges.

Leaders and other staff share responsibility for the creation, operation and long-term effectiveness of this inclusive culture. Leaders need to encourage and welcome contributions from all staff and ensure their suggestions and efforts are valued and recognized.

In turn, staff need to contribute positively to the forming and implementation of change and actively show they understand and support a culture where opportunities are explored and challenges are faced in a professional and effective manner.

From this base, a common understanding develops that all major challenges can be overcome by combining the right talent within the organization with the appropriate remodelling approach. When such a commitment to cultural change is fully embedded, the sense of all-staff empowerment and positive attitude to change and progress becomes the organization's default setting – the way it meets all challenges and opportunities.

> As the change process is largely driven by the views and insights of front-line workers and young people, there is a real sense shared by all involved that the solutions will be effective and sustainable. The process is largely bottom up and this has really helped deepen understanding of what, why and where the problems affecting young people in our area are and what we can do to address them. Our five change teams are in the middle of developing solutions as I write. (Rita Chohan, Project Coordinator, Target Youth Support pathfinder, Leicester City, 2006)

This capacity minimizes possible disruption and allows organizations to embrace and manage change while remaining focused on their core business.

A key benefit of remodelling over many other change management processes is that it is not a top-down model. While it depends on the commitment of the senior leadership team, remodelling is inclusive and engages and empowers all staff to have a direct involvement in leading change, problem solving and developing solutions.

> Everyone has the opportunity to contribute to remodelling activities, including governors and parents. (Eddie Thomas, former headteacher, Cheetwood Primary School, Manchester, 2005)

Organizations that are still dominated by hierarchical structures and industrial-age thinking can find this model difficult to accept. However, as the vast majority of leadership and management thinkers predict, this will have to change if these organizations are to survive, and lead and manage change, in today's knowledge society.

Constructive collaboration

Remodelling promotes and is underpinned by the development of constructive communication and working practices between organizations and their stakeholders. Throughout schools in England, for example, where remodelling has become a way of life, new partnerships are developing and language is changing between key stakeholders, the wider community and partner organizations.

The growing belief in collaboration between schools has partly been driven by the national agenda, but there is also an increasing belief among those leading schools that remodelling is a constructive way forward and that it presents everyone with a win-win scenario.

While the priorities of schools change, and their strategies and solutions vary, they are finding great value in collaborating and sharing experiences, ideas and solutions with their staff and with agencies and other schools and organizations – local and nationally.

Collaboration, of course, can take many forms – as with all aspects of remodelling no one size fits all. Active collaboration between individuals and between organizations can range from relatively informal arrangements, where resources, knowledge and experiences are shared, to semi-formal networks or formal federations.

Whatever form it takes, it is important that collaboration takes place during each stage of every significant change project. This should, when appropriate and useful, include working with other groups and organizations external to the organization or organizations directly involved in the change process.

Collaborating organizations should also ensure a defined, proactive and effective process for ensuring that their stakeholders remain involved and updated on progress of their change process.

> The [school] federation is going to provide the pupils and the staff with greater opportunities to work together to tackle the challenges that we have in the area. It will further support the creation of teams at every level, which is vital if we are to pull together over the coming year. (Andrea Norris, headteacher, Langley Infant School, Plymouth, 2005)

Whatever its form, the active and constructive collaboration, that remodelling encourages, helps individuals and organizations meet numerous and varied challenges and embed a culture of openness to positive change.

Proactive and inclusive change team(s)

Proactive and inclusive remodelling change teams help organizations make informed and focused decisions, generate best possible solutions and implement sustainable and long-lasting changes.

Change teams include representatives from all staff areas – and other stakeholders, depending on the changes under consideration. For example, many schools include governors, parents and/or pupils in their change teams. Although they have many common factors, these teams can vary in composition, how and when they meet, roles and time commitments of members, and so on.

Inclusiveness is vital, as people in different roles have different and valuable views and ideas about change. They also have different cultural understandings and expectations. Sometimes change teams go through a difficult initial period as their members get used to the new way of working. Change teams require sound and patient leadership during this initial period.

Change teams enable people to support what they help to create. Broad involvement leads to better and more lasting improvements; it also helps everyone to clearly see and experience the benefits of remodelling. This is why one of the first actions of remodelling is setting up a representative change team that provides an open, honest and collaborative environment for active discussion on all aspects of change.

Change teams have a very profound and positive effect on organizational culture. For example, staff feel much more included and involved in the running of their organizations, and traditional hierarchical roles, such as the role of the managing director, change and become more inclusive to adapt to this.

This shift can involve a period of resistance to change. The openness and honesty of change teams is crucial to overcoming this resistance and encouraging the smooth development and implementation of changes.

Successful change teams quickly become an integral part of organizational life. They become the habitual way organizations make their decisions and implement changes – and all members of staff fully understand and appreciate their purpose, objectives and benefits.

However, change teams should be understood as project teams with a clear brief and a limited life span. They should not be set up with the objective of creating a new power base in an organization. They also need to have excellent communication channels and remain open to challenge.

> The other important outcome of this whole school day on remodelling was the formation of the school change team. We decided that, with a compact and unified school staff, no one should be denied the opportunity to sit on the change team and the

overwhelming majority of staff, both teaching and support, decided that they wanted to participate. I took the conscious decision not to be a member of the change team. Obviously I am kept informed about change team discussions and proposals, but I did not want to feel that I was inhibiting the process. The impact of the change team is making us look at future structures and systems within the school and the possibility that the senior management team might be replaced by the change team and a leadership team. (Sandra Mitchell, former headteacher Dove Bank Primary School, Staffordshire, 2005)

Change teams are a vital component of successful remodelling. The next chapter discusses the role of these teams in more depth.

Proven change process

To direct change and ensure it is positive, it is vital to have a vision, a strategy and a proven, structured and adaptable process for managing change in place, supported by appropriate skills and tools.

As previously stated, remodelling is a proven change process that enables organizations to develop effective and long-term change programmes that meet their specific circumstances. It's a generic and powerful process that produces unique made-to-measure outcomes by enabling and encouraging organizations and their partners to:

- identify and agree where change is needed;
- facilitate a vision of the future shared across the whole organization and stakeholder communities;
- collaborate internally and externally with other organizations and agencies, in an effective and productive way;
- create and implement plans for tailored change in an atmosphere of consensus;
- embed an inclusive and proactive culture of long-term progress;
- improve performance and standards for staff and stakeholders, including customers.

Rational, political and emotional considerations

The remodelling change process is designed to help organizations engage with all staff in a way that takes account of the rational, political and emotional aspects of change and achieve and embed positive developments (see Figure 5.2).

For changes to be sustainable and last into the long term, the rational, political and emotional factors that influence and are influenced by these changes need to be identified, managed and incorporated throughout the duration of the change process.

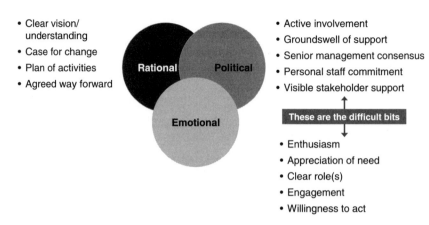

- Clear vision/ understanding
- Case for change
- Plan of activities
- Agreed way forward

Rational   Political

Emotional

- Active involvement
- Groundswell of support
- Senior management consensus
- Personal staff commitment
- Visible stakeholder support

These are the difficult bits

- Enthusiasm
- Appreciation of need
- Clear role(s)
- Engagement
- Willingness to act

Figure 5.2 Emotional and political barriers must be overcome before the rational solution can be accepted (TDA, 2007).

It is critical, therefore, that at each stage of the change process the change team and the leadership team are aware of and mindful of what all those involved in change are thinking, feeling, saying and doing.

This is not always an easy task. Most individuals and organizations are relatively adept at managing the rational aspects – the structural and organizational elements – of change, but not quite so good at managing the myriad, and not always all that rational, ways human beings view, react, adapt to and cope with change.

To achieve deep-seated and sustainable change and embed a culture that fosters continual progress, organizations must work with and manage the emotional and political aspects of change, as well as the rational.

When individual's feelings, preferences and political sensitivities are understood and respected, they feel valued and included and become enthusiastic co-creators and facilitators of positive change. When these factors are not respected, people can feel undervalued and excluded and they can become barriers to change.

Organizations and their change teams, therefore, need to give equal prominence to rational, political and emotional factors when discussing, leading and implementing change. In particular, they need to be aware of how the political and emotional aspects of change can potentially hinder or encourage success.

This awareness includes having a strong understanding of the importance and relevance of the change curve and the dip in motivation that is an inevitable part of real change.

Complexity

Organizational change is always a mix of the simple and the complex. Sometimes the changes that are made can be profoundly radical and sometimes they may seem almost pedestrian. But even when the changes appear minor, the contribution and adjustments – rational, political and emotional – made by individuals and organizations involved in the changes are always complex.

The remodelling change process directly reflects this pattern. At its core, it's a simple five-stage process that helps organizations to make fundamental and very positive changes in a way that minimizes disruption and maximizes benefits – both in terms of their cultures and their performance.

But, as discussed in this chapter, underpinning the remodelling process is a great wealth of complex method, experience and understanding. It's this depth and complexity that paradoxically ensures that the remodelling process, in itself, gives organizations the support and direction they require to develop and implement all the changes and solutions they need to make smoothly, easily and, most importantly, productively – into the long term.

6 Remodelling: the change team

The remodelling change management process enables individuals and organizations to address issues collaboratively and come up with made-to-measure solutions – one size doesn't fit all – and produce sustainable plans, actions and outcomes. To put it more simply, remodelling helps organizations direct and manage change and adapt, develop and succeed into the long term.

Remodelling takes organizations through the staged process that Harvard business school professor and change expert, John Kotter (see Chapter 4, 1996), says is vital if organizations are to manage change successfully. It enables them to: establish a sense of urgency; create a guiding coalition; develop a vision and strategy; communicate the change vision; empower a broad base of people to take action; generate short-term wins; consolidate gains and produce even more change; and anchor the new approaches into the culture.

Most remodelling organizations report that the single most powerful of these key aspects of successful change, and the one that in many ways makes all the others possible, is the creation and operation of a 'guiding coalition'. This is why the single most vital part of the remodelling change management process is developing and running inclusive and collaborative change teams.

John Kotter states that members of guiding teams – change teams – need to possess: '. . . credibility, skills, connections, reputations and formal authority required to provide changed leadership. This group learns to operate . . . with trust and emotional commitment' (1996, page 4).

In addition, change teams need to include a range of people from all areas and levels of an organization or organizations. The importance and impact of moving to this more collaborative and inclusive approach to change and style of leadership – and so, ultimately, to a more inclusive organizational culture – is evidenced by a recent independent PricewaterhouseCoopers' study looking into the implications of remodelling on leadership in schools.

The study found clear evidence that schools and school leaders need to change radically to cope with the increasingly diverse demands they are facing. In particular, PricewaterhouseCoopers (2007) strongly recommends greater diversification of leadership to help share the increased responsibilities of all the changes that are taking place in schools. This includes, for example, improvements to school improvement planning, the development of extended services such as breakfast and after-school clubs, swift and easy access to additional support, and engaging parents more in pupil learning and working towards social cohesion in local communities.

Inclusive and collaborative change teams help schools and other organizations to successfully achieve this diversified leadership. These teams also enable organizations to make informed and focused decisions, generate best possible solutions and implement sustainable and long-lasting changes.

As previously mentioned, change teams need to include representatives from all staff departments, or, when a number of different organizations are involved, from all of the organizations (for example, targeted youth support). Although change teams share a great many common factors, they tend to vary in composition, how and when they meet, the roles and time commitments of members, and so on.

Of course, most organizations already have active staff committees and teams. But generally these bodies are not fully representative of all staff groups and do not operate in the fully inclusive and collaborative way that change teams do. They also tend to be long term, whereas change teams are short term, created to address specific issues over a set timeframe. Where existing groups are truly working inclusively and collaboratively it makes sense to build on this good practice.

Some of the information in this chapter is also available online at www.tda.gov.uk/remodelling.aspx

Inclusiveness

Change teams have a profound effect on organizational culture. For example, staff feel more included and involved in the running of organizations and feel more of a sense of ownership (both of the change process itself and of the changes that are made). People support what they help to create. Staff work more as a team and their morale and motivation increases as a result, often with a positive effect on performance and productivity – as well as on other related issues such as recruitment and retention.

The inclusiveness of change teams is vital, as involving a wide range of people (and roles) encourages a wide range of viewpoints, understandings, innovative ideas and solutions.

> This has been a major benefit of the remodelling process. The way it works drives this change, there's nowhere to hide. Some of this benefit has simply been in awareness

raising – in changing the perception of people about the need for change. Staff now understand this need – and this is helping us to develop more targeted training programmes, not least to help us managers do an even better job and work even more effectively with our employer partners. (Kevin Cleaver, Head of Hospitality and Leisure, Lewisham Further Education College)

People in different roles and departments (and in different organizations) have varied and very valuable insights, views and ideas about the current situation and about changes that need implementing. Broad involvement leads to better and more lasting improvements. It also helps everyone to see clearly and experience the benefits of remodelling.

Remodelling the workforce is different for each school, but working as a cluster has enabled us to explore a range of ideas, ask questions and begin to find some answers together. (Julia Carey, Lostwithiel primary school, Boconnoc cluster, Lostwithiel)

This is why one of the first actions of the remodelling change process is setting up a representative change team – generally involving a completely new mix of staff or organizations – that provides an open, honest and collaborative environment for the active discussion of all aspects of change.

Among other benefits, this new mix of staff or organizations results in:

- Creating a blend of knowledge and skills that encourages creative thinking, holistic solutions and collective ownership of the issues.
- Generating effective information sharing between individuals or organizations, focused on clear aims and outcomes.
- A growing understanding of each other's departments or organizations and the links or potential links between them.
- The development of a shared understanding of each other's way of working and appreciation of each other's issues, challenges and aims. This can include, particularly when a number of organizations is involved in a change team, the development of a shared language and an appreciation and understanding of each other's way of working.
- Collaborative working – within the change teams, within the organization(s) as a whole, and with customers/clients.
- Breaking down cultural barriers and a more holistic approach to forming solutions.
- Identifying previously unrecognized factors leading to poor outcomes, by drilling down into issues in depth.
- Identifying efficiencies through sharing resources and infrastructure, providing cost savings and efficiency gains by avoiding duplication.
- The identification of quick wins – easy to implement changes that can be carried out right away, independent of the overall change plan. These help maintain a high level of commitment and enthusiasm for the change project.

- Having a clear mandate and decision-making capability.
- A shared vision that helps bring together existing plans, while not comprising people's individual aims and outcomes.
- Shared goals and objectives.
- Increased continual professional development opportunities for all staff.

New teams require attention to ensure that they work effectively. Thought needs to be given, for example, as to how to encourage the full contribution of each member of the team, and make sure that everyone understands what each person brings to the team and agrees how best to work together.

> It's a novel experience working on a change team. It took a while to get used to it. It was definitely empowering, but some of the team had to get over having senior managers in the room. To begin with these managers tried to dominate a bit. But as we all settled down things relaxed and we all took an equal part in the team. (Kevin Cleaver, Head of Hospitality and Leisure, Lewisham Further Education College)

Change teams also need the full support of senior staff (outside of the teams) so they know that their work and proposed changes will be treated seriously.

The time demands of team membership also need to be considered and team members' work/life balance must be respected. In addition, an effective monitoring process needs to be set up to assess the work and progress of the team throughout the change process. It is also important that clear accountability processes are put in place from the outset.

Setting up a change team

Change teams are set up at the start of the remodelling change process. There are exceptions to this, though, as the process is tailored to each specific change situation and requirement.

Multi-agency project teams were set up by the targeted youth support pathfinders at the start of the remodelling process to manage and drive the change. These teams did not include members of all stakeholder organizations at the beginning. It was argued that this was because, when a group of organizations is involved, a core group of key organizations needs to start a remodelling project before involving all stakeholders.

All stakeholder groups were, however, engaged very early on in the targeted youth support change processes, and involved and consulted throughout the first three stages of the process – before becoming active change team members in the develop and deliver stages.

The targeted youth support change teams were made up of representatives from a mix of agencies and groups crucial to delivering targeted youth support, including housing, district councils and transport, the police, Connexions, schools, the youth service, youth offending teams, voluntary agencies, community workers, parents and young people.

As well as differences in timing, there can also be variations in the number of change teams that are set up. Most organizations usually have one team, but sometimes, when organizations are particularly large and/or complex or when a range of organizations are working on a change programme together, a number of change teams is set up to look at different aspects of change – for example, to explore solutions to different individual challenges. When this is the case, these change teams liaise with each other and with the staff groups or organizations that they represent, and usually report to a steering group.

As organizations take a remodelling approach to all change into the long term, new change teams are often set up to address specific issues, as and when necessary, after the initial change process has ended its first cycle.

Change teams need to be fully representative of all of an organization's staff groups – or, when a number of organizations are involved in a change project, of all the key organizations involved in and affected by the project. The exact composition of change teams depends on the specific change project and local decisions, arrived at democratically.

> We formed our change team by taking all our staff away for the day. We also invited school governors and people from our LEA [local education authority]. The idea was to set up a structure where all areas were represented. Since then we've modified the change team and restructured it so only key people attend. Today, we have individual change teams for specific activities. (Mary Nicholls, headteacher of Forest Hall Primary School, North Tyneside)

It isn't necessary to have all staff on the change team though; rather, the objective is to form a team that brings everyone's voice into the room. The best way to achieve this is to create team membership that looks like a diagonal slice through the organization – for example, some managers, some backroom and frontline staff, and perhaps some customers (in schools, customers are pupils, parents and often community members). It is important to avoid simply inviting the usual suspects. Essentially, a well balanced and effective change team:

- is made up of the 'right' people, representative of all departments and levels within an organization or organizations;
- gives and receives feedback openly and constructively;
- remains focused on its remit;
- engages actively with a range of customers to ensure that their views are fully incorporated into solutions;

- is bold in actively engaging relevant stakeholders – and pulling new people into the team when there is a gap and a need;
- has a real creative buzz to its meetings. There is real passion to make a difference;
- has at least one member who is skilled in facilitation and familiar with the remodelling tools and techniques;
- has at least one member who has been involved in a change process before.

Change teams need to be of a manageable size (enabling everyone to input) and be able and prepared to meet on a regular basis throughout a change project. Some change teams meet on a weekly or monthly basis; others organize fewer more intensive sessions to accomplish their work.

It is advisable to ensure that a range of personalities – as well as roles – is well represented in the change team. This is important as it encourages a diversity of contributions. A truly inclusive team builds better solutions. It is important to be creative and flexible about how people contribute to the work of change teams. Not everyone is able to make the same commitment.

Through strong and ongoing communication, both within the team and with staff groups outside the team, change teams develop a shared vision of what to achieve and the changes needed to do it. The remodelling tools and techniques help all staff get involved in developing strategies and solutions critical to any change initiative.

To be effective, the remit and expectations of change teams need to be discussed and set as early as possible. This includes having a specific focus for the change team that can be adapted to address any new objectives as and when necessary, and creating time limits – often in the form of milestones – for the operation and targets of the change team.

Leading change teams

Remodelling change teams encourages an inclusive democratic leadership culture, so it is vital that senior staff do not attempt to lead them in an autocratic way. Nonetheless, an individual or group does often need to take responsibility to coordinate the efforts of the team – especially early on in the change process before the team has built its own momentum.

Facilitation is a vital role. Change team members often nominate a different member of the team to facilitate each of its meetings. A good change team facilitator encourages debate among the change team in a positive and constructive way, ensures everyone has a say, and has an open mind about what the outcome of any debate might be. The facilitator needs to keep the team focused on its remit and deliverables, encourage innovative thinking and ensure that the team uses the remodelling tools and techniques in a creative way.

Rational, political, emotional

For a change project to succeed, the rational, political and emotional aspects that influence change need to be identified, managed and incorporated throughout the project. This includes ensuring that all involved staff develop an awareness of the importance and relevance of the emotional curve they experience during the change process (for more details of the change curve see Chapter 4).

The remodelling process helps change teams support and engage all staff throughout a change project in a way that takes account of these emotional, political and rational factors, and achieves and embeds positive long-term change.

The start of the remodelling process can invoke an initial period of resistance to change. The inclusiveness, openness and honesty of change teams are key to overcoming this resistance and encouraging the smooth development and implementation of changes.

To ensure success, change team meetings need to be well planned and facilitated, and should provide a focus where ideas and issues are progressed through deploying remodelling skills and tools.

Successful change teams quickly become an integral part of an organization's life; and all members of staff fully understand and appreciate their purpose, objectives and benefits. These teams become the habitual way organizations make their decisions and implement changes.

Change teams in the public sector

Remodelling can be successfully adapted to virtually any change situation in both the private and public sector. As the process is currently being deployed on a national scale in the public sector – enabling local authorities, further education colleges, schools and a broad range of other agencies and services that support children and young people, to successfully change, work more collaboratively and improve – the following sections will discuss the work of change teams in public sector organizations, particularly schools.

While members of school change teams are predominantly (and often exclusively) school staff, it does not require a great a leap of imagination to see their roles as equivalent to those in other organizations in both the public and private sector. For example, the headteacher is clearly a director of services or a managing director or CEO, a school governor is a member of the board, school managers are business managers, and teachers and support staff are comparable backroom and frontline parts of any organizations' main workforce.

The same equivalence is true for the way school change teams operate and their impact on the ways schools run.

Attributes of school change teams

Many schools already have teams to help facilitate progress and improvement, but these teams tend to work within the existing school culture and usually comprise senior leaders and perhaps some teachers. School remodelling change teams operate well outside this structural status quo and so really foster a positive culture change in schools.

> The real bonus for us has been having a school change team, which has involved people from across the school in the decision-making process – staff members really feel their views are being listened to. (Nick Jones, Highfield Junior and Infant School, Birmingham)

Effective school change teams are made up of an inclusive staff group, including representatives of teaching and support staff and, where possible, pupils, parents, governors, unions representatives, agencies and other local organizations (the membership of change teams is discussed in more detail later in this chapter). Change team members take responsibility for leading change through the remodelling process.

They do not take sole responsibility, though. Each change team member involves his or her departmental colleagues in making and implementing change team decisions, providing them with feedback at regular meetings and asking for their input. In effect, each representative acts as a dynamic communications channel between the change team and the rest of the workforce, representing their own views and the views of those not on the team.

Where appropriate, it is also important that change teams and schools collaborate with other schools, external stakeholders and partner organizations. The advent of the extended school agenda, for example, is encouraging more and more schools to collaborate not only with other schools, but also with other organizations, individuals and agencies, and tap into the richness of resources that exist in local communities.

To enable swift and easy access (to support vulnerable children and young people), for example, many schools are working collaboratively with social and health services, the police, the youth offending team, voluntary and community organizations and parents. Numerous schools also work with a critical friend – an external mentor with experience of remodelling.

Change teams have a very profound and positive effect on school culture. School staff are more included and involved in the running of their schools. They feel more of a sense of ownership and work more as a team, and their morale and motivation increases as a result – with a very positive effect on standards of teaching and learning, and ultimately on pupil outcomes.

Remodelling stages and school change teams

As mentioned earlier, change teams are generally set up at the beginning of the remodelling change process. The work of these teams develops as the five distinct but often overlapping stages of the TDA process – mobilize, discover, deepen, develop and deliver – unfold. For example:

- During the mobilize stage, inclusive school change teams with decision-making capabilities are set up, and clear communication and reporting channels are developed.
- During the discover stage, change teams focus on uncovering issues around school priorities, identifying what is working well as well as issues that need addressing.
- During the deepen stage, change teams acquire a greater understanding of the scale and scope of the changes they need to make, and the challenges involved. They use the remodelling process and its tools to identify the root causes of issues, establish those that are causing or have the potential to cause the most problems, and clarify which staff members may be and/or are most affected. They also analyse how solutions and strategies might be developed. Some issues may necessitate forming sub-teams – often directly involving people from outside the change team, drawing on the depth of knowledge and understanding of others. Change teams may also implement some quick wins during this stage.
- During the develop stage, change teams use remodelling problem-solving techniques to develop made-to-measure, effective and sustainable strategies and solutions to address the highest priority issues. An implementation plan is developed to deliver these solutions. What emerges is a shared view of the future and the changes needed to get there. Communication across the whole school is particularly vital during this stage as the thinking about solutions evolves.
- During the deliver stage, change teams start to implement (and/or oversee the implementation of) the changes they have developed. The time it takes to implement these changes depends on the complexities of each individual change project.

As discussed in Chapter 3, the remodelling change process also has an implicit sixth stage, sustain. It embeds a proactive and collaborative culture where individuals and organizations – in this case schools and school staff – have the skills, experience, confidence and commitment to apply an effective remodelling approach to all significant challenges at all times into the long term.

Change team case study: Banbury School, Oxfordshire

As a large secondary school with over 1,700 pupils, Banbury has a large teaching staff and even more support staff. Because of this, the school started off its remodelling process in two separate presentation meetings. These meetings were followed by brainstorming sessions designed to highlight issues in the school.

Membership of a school change team

The membership of school change teams varies from school to school and according to the specific focus of each change project. Typically, they include a mix of school leaders, classroom teachers, extended schools coordinators, teaching assistants and other support staff, premises and facilities management staff, governors, pastoral care staff, pupils and parents.

In small schools, change teams generally involve all members of staff; in larger schools, change teams are usually made up of representatives from all staff areas.

When we entered the remodelling process, we formed a change team that consisted of the entire staff of the school. It's one of the things that we most love about the process, everyone working together and feeling involved. (Melanie Hinson, headteacher of Whalton Primary School in Northumberland)

Where school change teams are working on a wider remit, for example, when they are looking at how best to develop extended services in and around schools, they may well also include members of local communities and representatives from local agencies and organizations, including the local authority, partners in the Children's Trust and local businesses.

The specific roles that people take in school change teams vary from team to team and school to school. Nonetheless, it is insightful to look at the roles that different school staff often take, with the strong caveat that this is very far from always the case. As mentioned earlier, these school staff roles are equivalent to roles found in most other organizations and businesses.

Headteachers do not usually sit on the change team as they almost inevitably inhibit and dominate the way it works – not least as a key outcome of an effective change team is the development of a culture of more distributed leadership. This 'letting go' is not always easy for headteachers and they can experience a period of uncertainty before they get used to, and benefit from, the new way of working.

Many headteachers who have been through the remodelling change process remark on what initially can feel like the significant wrench of losing total control of their school and handing over many of their leadership duties to their school colleagues. These headteachers generally follow up this comment by listing the benefits of this letting go – for examples, reduced workload and reduced stress, the satisfaction of watching others develop, and the pure practical benefit of having more time to think and plan at a more strategic level.

I think this school is better led by a wider leadership group, involving people from all levels. Devolved leadership results in better decision making as decisions are made by people who are directly involved in the issues and directly affected by the changes. (Peter Laurence, Brigshaw High School and Language College)

Headteachers usually choose to input their ideas into school change teams in the same way as other school staff. As they have ultimate responsibility for their schools, it is important that headteachers are aware of how well change teams are working. Regular reports, formal and informal, from change teams to headteachers are therefore a necessity.

Senior leaders (other than headteachers) often take an active facilitation role in change teams as they usually have practical experience as facilitators. Theirs is a delicate role, as they need to take a strategic view and link to the headteacher without dominating the team and without seeming like, or being, the headteacher's stooge.

It is usually not wise, therefore, for senior leaders to chair school change teams. Many senior leaders choose to take a back-seat role and give input as required. Their presence alone helps give change teams confidence that they are taken seriously.

Classroom teachers' understanding of their pupils' needs and aspirations is vital to keeping a strong focus of change teams on the key goal of improving standards of teaching and learning. Teachers also have a clear understanding of the workload and work/life balance implications of any potential changes on their peers. This is particularly important for two reasons: one, workload and work/life balance are key issues for teachers and increasing their workload in any way is simply not acceptable; and, two, their presence in change teams helps ensure buy-in from other teachers, the core staff group of any school.

Teaching assistants, higher level teaching assistants and other support staff also have a very close understanding of pupils' needs and aspirations. Their perspective tends to be different from that of classroom teachers, as they work in a different way with pupils (often one-to-one, for example) and they are more likely to live in the communities that pupils come from and often know the pupils' parents and families. The insights that come from this personal perspective are very valuable to the work of change teams.

Support staff are a key part of the school workforce and are becoming increasingly important. They are fast approaching 50 per cent of the workforce and are working in around 60 different and distinct roles. Their views are hugely important and change teams should always contain at least one support staff member. As with teachers, the implication of all potential changes on their workload and work/life balance needs to be considered and discussed.

Extended schools coordinators are becoming increasingly important members of change teams, as developing extended services is now a core task for all schools – and change teams are often a key mechanism that enables them to do their job well. Developing extended services often involves changing long-established school structures, and change teams help input creatively into these changes and deal in a positive way with any initial resistance from staff to changing how 'we've always done things'.

Extended schools coordinators usually have a good understanding of how other schools are approaching the development of extended services. As local schools often work together to provide these services, extended schools coordinators frequently represent a cluster of schools. This wider perspective is extremely valuable.

Premises managers are also becoming increasingly important members of change teams, as schools are now being used by a wider range of people, for a wider range of activities, over longer hours. Premises managers' understanding of practical issues around how and when the buildings can be used is invaluable. Any extensions to the use of school buildings also can have a direct impact on these managers' workload and they need to be involved in all discussions about this.

Bursars/school business managers can give practical advice and guidance on what is possible from a financial perspective. They also generally have good links with organizations and businesses outside schools and these contacts can be extremely useful, for example when developing extended services. They have also been trained in risk management and may well have access to simple but effective tools for managing risk. Not all schools have bursars and business managers, but the role is becoming more and more widespread.

Parents bring a deeper understanding of parental needs and their children's lives into school change teams. They also often bring a range of specialist skills and experience to the teams. Their involvement reinforces the message that parents and schools are partners in the education of their children.

It is important that parents' views are considered. It is also important that parents understand what the school (and change team) is setting out to achieve and the implication of any changes. It is important to put processes in place that enable parents on the change team to liaise with and feedback to all parents.

The TDA has developed a consultation toolkit targeted at parents, pupils and their communities (regarding extended services). It also contains learnings for other consultations. It is available at www.tda.gov.uk/upload/resources/pdf/c/consultationtoolkit.pdf

Pupils are included in change teams in a way that is appropriate to their age group, school and the issues being addressed. This may, for example, involve occasional involvement in change team meetings or the setting up of a separate pupil change team that is able to feed their ideas and reactions into the main school change team. Care needs to be taken to ensure that a full range of all pupils' views are captured and considered.

Involving pupils helps change teams to balance pupils' desires and needs more accurately. It also helps change teams incorporate pupils' emotional considerations into any changes and avoids a purely clinical approach to outcomes. In addition, it helps build a culture of pupil participation and ownership in schools, which can have a very positive effect on behaviour, learning and outcomes.

Governors help give overall strategic context to the work of change teams and help ensure the teams' work is taken seriously. They also create a strong link between the governing body and the practical considerations of changes in the school. In addition, they are often able to advise on the legal and financial liabilities of potential changes.

Agencies and services are working more and more with schools, for example, in collaborative teams that ensure vulnerable children and young people get identified and supported as early as possible, usually within the school, context (the swift and easy access requirement of the extended services agenda).

Agencies and services bring a great breadth of experience and a different perspective to school change teams. This has many benefits, for example: it ensures the change team contains a great deal of specialist knowledge (this can accelerate the change process and make changes even more effective); it raises awareness that schools are not working alone towards improving outcomes; it reveals where collaborative working is and can be most effective; it helps identify mutually supportive service goals; and it often brings quick wins.

Personal perspectives of a change team – Brigshaw High School and Language College

Brigshaw High School and Language College is a comprehensive school of approximately 1,400 pupils, serving the former mining communities to the south-east of Leeds, in West Yorkshire. It first set up a change team five years ago as part of its remodelling change process, to help it develop and implement the requirements of the National Agreement with an aim to raise educational standards.

The team accomplished this task successfully. Although the team was disbanded once its work around the National Agreement was completed, the school was so impressed with the team's impact and the overall remodelling approach to change, and the knock-on benefits this has had, that it has subsequently set up a number of change teams to address specific issues. The school has used a change team and remodelling approach to a number of whole school issues – changes to catering and dining arrangements; pupil guidance and support; developing the role of governors; and identifying school improvement priorities.

Principal Peter Laurence says: 'We run the school very much on a remodelling approach.'

Brigshaw currently has a change team looking at improving the 'whole dining experience for pupils', which builds on the good work the school has already done around nutritional standards. Issues it is addressing include creating more dining space, reducing queuing times, improving seating arrangements, extending the kitchen, introducing new automatic payment cards and running the whole catering service more commercially.

The commercial potential of the catering service is very important to the school as it is an important source of revenue that is used to fund additional teaching and learning projects, helping drive standards up still further.

The school's aim is to create such an excellent all-round dining experience that all pupils choose to have lunch in the school (currently some pupils choose to go to local shops or to a local burger bar). In addition, the change team is also looking at plans to extend the catering facilities to tempt in outside customers, for example opening in the evening to cater for adult education and sports classes.

The change team includes a number of catering staff including the catering manager, support staff, the facilities manager, an assistant principle, three pupils and a teacher. Here, a cross-section of these staff explain, in their own words, their experiences of being on the change team.

Simon Lenners (Catering Manager)

'It's a really positive experience being in the change team and to have representatives from all parts of the school involved. This is a really good thing as we get the widest scope possible of opinions and priorities, not least from pupils. This helps breaks down barriers, encourages everyone to communicate and gives everyone a sense of ownership.

'I regularly talk with my 17 staff to ensure all of their views are included in what we discuss in the change team meetings – then I feed back what has been decided in the meetings to them. I do the same with pupils – they are our customers after all. It's important to discuss ideas with them and take on board their thoughts, and not just do what we adults think is right for them.

'I think I bring a realistic view of what's possible into the change team. I keep open to ideas and different ways of approaching things. It's great to hear others' points of view – often it's an entirely different take to my own and this leads to new ideas. Even if something isn't possible we look for a way to make it happen in some form or other.

'Strictly speaking, I'm a contract caterer, but I've been here for six years so I know the school well. Being on the change team has made me feel much more part of the Brigshaw team. It's helped to make me feel even more valued. My catering services management came to one meeting. They were really impressed and are very happy to support Brigshaw to improve things.

'It's great for my team to get involved – they feel more valued too. It's helped break down the "they are only kitchen staff" attitude. Mind you, staff here were never really like that, but it's certainly helped pupils see us as people and communicate with us more.

'I see this as a long-term thing. I think it'll increase the profile of the catering staff. People see there's something happening, the students in particular, and they realize that we are here to serve and help them. They also realize the limitations we're working too. We get more respect as a result.'

Martine H, Michaela B and Jack H (students and school council members)

'The change team is great as you can see all different points of view. It is also really good not to be overlooked like we sometimes are. I find it genuinely interesting. I talk to other pupils to tell them what's going on and to tell them what we're doing.'

'The staff in the change team make it easy for us to speak – in fact I think we probably speak the most! There's a real feeling that we're making things happen; and that feels really good. I've a sense of pride knowing I've suggested something that's going to actually happen.'

'It's still early days but already I feel more included in what's going on in the school. For example, we suggested having round tables rather than rectangular so that no pupils feel left out sitting on the end. We're going to have a look at some samples this afternoon. It makes me realize that it's not as difficult to change things as I thought. There's a sense of ownership. It's not just pupils and staff in two separate groups. The change team has given me a sense of us working together as one body.'

'We bring the pupils' voice to the change team. The adults would be guessing without us. For example, they had some ideas to start with and, to be honest, quite a few of them weren't quite right. We were able to tell them what pupils really want. It lets staff see how pupils feel about the school. I think they treat us differently as a result. I feel more valued, I feel they value my opinion. I'm also more appreciative of their work. For example, I can see just how hard the catering job is and now, rather than hardly noticing the kitchen staff, I see them as individual people who I can chat to.'

'The change team has made things seem more collective. There are only three of us on the change team, but we represent the opinions of all pupils. We chat with our friends and stuff and talk on the school council, so we know what people don't like and what they want. Most of the time we can tell the staff what's really happening.'

'I like it now when people say something to me about lunchtimes, particularly if it's a moan. It's great to say we're getting it sorted. It's really satisfying. I enjoy being asked about things. You genuinely feel like you matter. I'm keen to get involved in other change teams.'

'The change team has made me feel more confident that I matter, and given me more confidence to speak to new people – pupils and staff. I think it'll help me for stuff in the future, maybe for what I want to do in life. I think it's also had a good effect on my school work as, when you tell teachers what you're doing, they look at you differ-ently. They feel you're making a difference and they have more respect. I was nervous to begin with in the change team, I still am sometimes, but I soon warm up once the meetings get going. Everyone is really helpful and encouraging. They take your ideas seriously.'

'One thing I've realized from the change team is that the whole issue with lunchtime is more complex than I thought. I know what it's like for staff now. We need to be a bit patient. It'd be good to visit some other schools and see how they do things.'

Janet Purcell (Office Manager)

'The change team has a good cross-section of staff and pupils from all levels. We started off with some brainstorming to find ideas. We all inputted into this and it was very successful. We're working very well together.

'Although there's not much hierarchy at this school, working in this team helps break down whatever hierarchy there is. It breaks down that barrier. We're aware an assistant principal is with us, for example, but it doesn't feel like he has any more seniority than us in the team.

'I'm working in the office, but I also do some supervision of mealtimes as I want to meet the pupils. I can bring a perspective from both these areas to our change team meetings and discussions.

'I speak for the support staff team, so I make sure I talk and feedback to them as often as I can. I think we are already pretty good with our meals – they're healthy and well prepared – but there are areas about the whole dining experience that could be improved. For example, the queues are too long and there's not enough seating. We're talking about putting a conservatory in so we can make more room. There are plenty of issues. Another area that's of big interest to support staff is extending the catering service to the evenings. If this happens we want to make sure it works for us and our needs are considered.

'We all feel included in the change team. No one feels left out and we all have a voice. The pupils on the team are great. One big thing I've learnt from them is the importance of the dining area as a social area. It's where everyone comes together. This has great significance for school team-building, for developing a sense of the school community as a whole.'

Stuart Clark (Facilities Manager)

'I take a business planning perspective to the change team. We want to improve the dining experience for pupils, but I need to ensure that what we come up with fits in the premises development plan and within our financial constraints. I'm also an intermediary between the various outside stakeholders – the catering company, furniture providers, and so on.

'One of the first things that was made clear in the team was that there was no such thing as a bad idea. I think this put everyone at ease. No matter how bizarre our ideas are they are treated with respect and discussed. This is important. Not so much for me as I'm pretty outgoing in these situations, but for some of the team members who aren't so used to this sort of thing it's really helpful. It's a good relaxed and informal atmosphere in team meetings too, which helps.

'I thought I knew what most of the issues were when I joined the team. But there's certainly been a lot of development through getting everyone involved; through seeing all their different viewpoints. Some of my ideas have been knocked back and some taken forwards. It's a very practical approach.

'There's a danger that this sort of team involvement can smack of tokenism in some schools. But here we have a genuine input and our decisions have weight. There's an end result – we can see it from idea to implementation. For pupils this is particularly important as they need to see they can have an effect. It gives them a sense of ownership of the project. Also they are influencers. They influence their peers. And if we want things to be a success this is a necessity. They input into the changes and sell them to others. They also know what's going on. Some of the best ideas come from gossip or informal chats – from corridor meetings and out in the playground. The change team is a way of hearing and capturing these conversations and capitalizing on them.

'The change team gives an opportunity for people in all walks of school life to feed into changes. It breaks down barriers. Everybody is able to see and hear each other's side of the story. It's very motivating. I'm pretty nosey and genuinely interested in improving the school and this is a great way to do it. It's empowering. It also makes you very accountable. If something is decided then you need to sort it and quickly, it's very visible. I get a real buzz from it.

'The team also increases my awareness of other departments that I might not necessarily get in touch with in my regular job. It helps me to recognize the key players in making change happen. It also helps me feel more supported as there are others involved. You can get blinkered if all you do is stay in your own work area or comfort zone. This gives you a broader view. It's also good for relationships as it encourages communication. Being involved in the team involves some extra effort but I know the benefits far outweigh the extra input.

'When pupils get involved in specific projects like this we see better behaviour and I think it improves attendance. It's about making a contribution. They feel more valued and this has a knock-on effect. It's a developing community where people look out for each other.'

Debbie Simpson and Lynn Hippey (Catering Assistants)

'It's really good to be involved in the change team. It's us who know how the kitchen works, after all. And we get all the other kitchen staff's opinions and the pupils' feedback on the food and queuing and so on. Being on the change team has really helped me feel part of the whole school staff. I feel I belong now, whereas before it sometimes felt as if catering didn't matter.'

'Lunchtime is very much a social time for young people. Hearing them talk about this on the team really helps me to appreciate the importance of our job much more. I hadn't really thought about it before. Now I do more to be more warm and welcoming to pupils. If they are shy, for example, I'll talk to them. It's helped me develop a more friendly connection with the children and with staff all through the school. I feel I can speak more openly and I feel more valued. I enjoy my job that much more, too. I like to be listened to.'

'We had a problem with pupils taking free dinners off other children by stealing their numbers. This meant we were giving away two dinners for the price of one. We were losing money and it was embarrassing to challenge the pupils who'd done nothing wrong. We came up with the idea of a photocard in the change team and it looks like this is going to happen. This feels really good. We're also talking about introducing an automatic cash card, but this depends on funding.'

'I like to organize things. Before I had my own children I was a manager. I haven't been using these skills in school, but now I am. I feel more involved as a result and I'm using skills that were being wasted. It's also giving me a chance to input into school plans in a bigger way – for example by developing our catering service into the evening.'

Chris Swales (Assistant Principal)

'We shortened the school lunch-break a while ago and we introduced more healthy food. So before we set up the change team we'd already made some changes and improvements. But it was clear that there was plenty more to do and we felt the best way to approach this would be to have a change team.

'To begin with I came up with some ideas I'd seen in other schools and thought they were pretty sound. I put these ideas to the team and very quickly found out that they weren't what the pupils wanted at all. This was quite a surprise and a learning experience for me. I thought pupils would want all sorts of activities to do at lunchtime, but they didn't, instead they wanted places to meet and chat. Because of this we're looking at getting some extra outside seating put in at the back of the gym. This is an easy thing to do and it's not expensive and as a spin-off it can be used during demonstrations in PE lessons.

'Catering is a huge issue in the school. We make a bigger proportion of our income from catering than any other school in the area. If we do even better we'll be able to afford more teachers, our pupils will be better off nutritionally, they will feel more ownership of the school – and this will improve behaviour and so on. Ultimately it'll improve standards. So catering is very much a key school improvement issue for us. This is part of our approach and this is why a change team is so important. It's inclusive, it ensures a student voice, and fully engages support staff and other staff. Our whole way of working as a school is very much consultative and bottom-up as we've found that this is the best way to get good results.

'I do some facilitation in the change team but I don't make decisions any more than anyone else. In fact they don't even look to me to make decisions. The expertise does not lie with me anyway. The others on the team are far closer to the issues.

'I bring an impartial view to the team I think. I provide the link to the school leadership team and governors and I'm able to give an overview with no bias. I think me being there gives the team confidence that it has the authority to do things. I also know what's financially possible – which saves time when a suggestion is simply not financially feasible.

'The students on the team are terrific. They are not at all inhibited and they have lots of good ideas. The same goes for everyone else, mind you. It's a really good atmosphere and, as well as being productive, the meetings are fun. By working in the team I get to meet people I wouldn't really meet otherwise, other than to say hello. It's really changed my opinion of what people have to offer. Everyone has really contributed. I think we should have even more of these teams in the future than we currently do.'

The principal's view

Principal Peter Laurence is not a member of the change team, but he follows its work closely . . . from a distance. He is careful not to take a direct leadership role.

'As a school, we believe in empowering people – pupils, teachers, support staff, parents and the community – whenever and wherever we can,' he says. 'To do that you have to let go of always being in control and give people real responsibility; and this is what the change team does.'

He explains how this links into another important school agenda, personalized learning, as the school's remodelling approach is about fitting the way it operates around the personal needs and wants of young people (and staff and other involved parties), rather than trying to fit young people (and staff and other involved parties) within the needs of the organization.

The school is working hard to develop more community links and links with other agencies and organizations that support young people. The aim is for it to become an integrated centre for children's services built around the needs of pupils. Taking a remodelling approach and involving these services in change teams is seen as the way to progress things successfully.

Peter Laurence says that remodelling and change teams have contributed significantly to improvements in the school. For example, exclusions have dropped by two-thirds over the past two years, an increasing number of students are staying on in education and training (over 80 per cent) and the number of ex-students not in education, employment or training is much lower than it was: only two students from the cohort of over 240 Year 11 leavers in 2007 are classified as not in education, employment and training (NEET). Staff absence is also significantly lower than the local authority average, the school is oversubscribed, and school results have improved year on year in most curriculum areas.

All of this represents substantial success for Brigshaw. The school serves a predominantly white, working-class area with, traditionally, a culture of low aspiration. Most of the parents, for example, went to the school themselves, and very few of them stayed on in the school after they were 16. Now around 50 per cent of students go on to the sixth form and a further 30 per cent of those that leave go on to further education. More and more students are also going on to universities, including Oxford and Cambridge.

'Ultimately, making these improvements is not all that complex. It's a lot to do with trust. It's about working from the bottom up. We think success is based on really high-quality relationships throughout the school and beyond. If you get that right there's no limit to what's possible. There's a really strong sense of belonging here, and much of this is due to our strong and inclusive remodelling culture and our openness to change. We go out of our way to foster this – hence our keenness for change teams,' says Peter Laurence.

7 Remodelling: the critical importance of leadership

At the heart of remodelling is an apparent paradox: that, while the remodelling change process involves devolved leadership and making it fully inclusive, strong senior leadership that supports the process is key to its success.

The resolution to this paradox lies in the insight and understanding of senior leaders. Their leadership during remodelling involves, in many ways, letting go of their leadership and sharing it with others. To put it more exactly: it involves them letting go of any vestiges of autocratic leadership that they may have been holding on to.

This involves trust and a willingness to take more risks. There is no doubt that the answers to many of the challenges the organization faces are already available within organizations. The issue is about listening. Too often leaders feel that they are appointed on the grounds that they, and only they, can resolve issues. Too often they believe that this is their duty and encourage others to believe it as well; and too often staff accept this belief and sit back waiting for instructions to deliver.

Time and time again, when changes are made under this style of leadership, they do not work – and very rarely are they sustainable. The reason is simple. The belief that leadership knows best leaves the great majority of workers feeling they have little to add, particularly if they are not asked. This wastes a huge amount of knowledge, skills and creativity. It also demotivates the workforce and severely limits organizational capacity.

From the outset, remodelling encourages leaders to recognize the creativity that exists within all staff and stakeholders. For the remodelling process to work effectively, leaders must be willing to let go of some control and engage the whole workforce and stakeholders directly in developing and implementing changes. This is a counter-cultural position where the tendency in times of turbulence is to revert to strong, charismatic leadership where a focus on measurable outcomes is the key and where those delivering the service are required to meet those targets or become dispensible.

Peter Senge, the author of *the Fifth Discipline* (2006) and a Professor at the Massachusetts Institute of Technology (MIT), redefines the role of leadership in the current climate:

> Leadership exists where people are no longer victims of circumstances but participate in creating new circumstances . . . it's not about position or power; it's not about accomplishments; it's ultimately not even about what we do. Leadership is about creating a domain in which human beings continually deepen their understanding of reality and become more capable of participating in the unfolding of the world. Leadership is about creating new realities. (page 3)

This underlying premise forms the basis of remodelling. It recognizes that human beings are not machines but highly creative animals, and that given the opportunity they will put their creativity to use for the benefit of the organization. Without the opportunity staff may comply and help meet targets, but they are very likely to be demotivated and disengaged.

In many cases, where leaders realize its potential, establishing an inclusive leadership approach is straightforward from the start of the remodelling process. In other instances, this may be one of the most profound outcomes of the remodelling process. Ultimately, successful remodelling demands a change to shared leadership.

Senior leaders do, though, have a key role in the remodelling process. In particular, it is them who say yes or no to proposed changes – they remain the ultimate arbiters of change. The difference is that they no longer come up with changes themselves without involving others in the formulation and development of these changes.

Usually, the new – remodelled – role of leaders is to enable others to come up with ideas. Leadership becomes fully focused on empowering the whole workforce, on capitalizing on all the skills and creativity it holds. In this technological age, where knowledge management and intellectual capital are the prime currency, this is key to ongoing organizational success.

> Leaders don't lead by position; they lead by inspiring trust and confidence. Leading through dynamic vision and motivation results in energy and progress. Leadership is a great responsibility, even more so in times of radical, system-wide change such as today. (Howard Kennedy, Director of Change, TDA, 2008b, page 5)

This type of leadership does not depend for its existence on hierarchy but on shared responsibility and accountability. Significantly, leadership becomes much more focused on coaching for improvement and succession planning to ensure sustainability is built into the system.

There are at least three current strategic areas that leaders, especially of public service organizations, need to focus on. These are:

- *Personalization*: strengthening the link between the client and service delivery by strengthening the link between the service and the requirements of the client. Simply put, creating a partnership base between the service and the client.
- *Modernization*: having the right people, with the necessary knowledge and skills, in the right place at the right time to enhance the service delivery to the identified needs of the client.
- *Partnership working*: recognizing that the organization cannot work alone to meet the needs of its customers. Traditionally, for example, both universal and targeted public services have both competed and jealously guarded their work areas. Through multi-agency working, the aim is to shift the focus of services onto the needs of the user and away from the needs of individual organizations.

The public sector needs to address the above three areas if the government's public sector agreements set out for 2008 to 2011 and beyond are to be met. Crucially, remodelling gives the sector the method and structure to successfully do this.

The private sector faces many of the same issues as the public sector. Without doubt, there is an opportunity for commercial organizations to learn from the remodelling that is happening in the public sector; around the huge changes that are going on in schools and in the development of more effective targeted youth support – and from the changes that are beginning to take place in the FE sector.

Energizing practice

In 2003 Tom Bentley and James Wilsdon of DEMOS argued for a new way of thinking in an adaptive state. An adaptive state is one in which the state recognizes the importance of people before policy in public service reform. It is a key stage in the adoption of a personalized agenda.

> Public services in diverse societies must offer far greater flexibility to meet personal needs, while keeping the ability to connect resources and activities across entire systems of governance. This is the only way to serve diverse needs equally well, and to make specialist knowledge and resources available to everybody. Services must also contribute to shared social contexts that enable people to thrive; performance within closed systems will be inadequate, however much improved.
>
> In other words, we need systems capable of continuously reconfiguring themselves to create new sources of public value. This means interactively linking the different layers and functions of governance, not searching for a static blueprint that predefines their relative weight. The central question is no longer how we can achieve precisely the right balance between different layers – central, regional and local – or between different sectors – public, private and voluntary. Instead, we need to ask *How can the system as a whole become more than the sum of its parts?* (Bentley and Wilsdon, 2003, page 16)

This is the new focus for leaders of the twenty-first century. The three key strategic areas are those identified earlier: personalization, workforce modernization and partnership working.

This book has already discussed workforce modernization and partnership working in some depth. It has also touched on personalization. Partnership working and personalization are such complex issues that they need some further examination here. While workforce modernization is also a complex issue it has already received a level of attention that suggests it need not be further addressed at this stage.

Personalization

Essentially, personalization means placing the user at the centre of delivery. The challenge for leaders is to recognize that everyone – customers, students, workers, service users – has different needs, different skills, and differing aptitudes, attitudes and aspirations.

The aim of personalization is, ultimately, to improve the performance of organizations. As Charles Leadbeater of 'think tank' DEMOS says about personalization in the public sector:

> By putting users at the heart of services, enabling them to become participants in the design and delivery, services will be more effective by mobilising millions of people as co-producers of the public goods they value. (2004, page 19)

It is important for organizations to develop an ethos that actively works towards personalization on an ongoing basis. In schools, for example, this means working in partnership with parents, pupils and others to create the flexibility and capability to develop personalization.

This increased personalization of service does not, of course, only apply to schools. It applies to virtually all public and private organizations. It requires a change in mindset, culture and behaviour that challenges long-held and prevalent assumptions, asks key questions and learns from experience.

Increased personalization is both challenging and rewarding for staff in organizations. It means new professional development needs, high e-learning skills, the deployment of advanced ICT capabilities, new chances for co-creation and greater democratization.

Leaders need to accept this change and help plan its delivery. However, they cannot do this on their own. They cannot presume they have the solutions. They do, though, have the capability to provide direction for solutions, both with their staff and with stakeholders who will benefit from the solutions.

The remodelling change process is a highly effective way of doing this. It provides the structure, tools and activities needed to develop personalization – tailored to fit each individual context. Remodelling also facilitates collaboration and partnership working, often in ways not imagined at the start of the process.

Collaboration and partnership working

Effective and sustainable change depends on the staff in organizations creating and sharing knowledge together, i.e. collaborating and working in partnership. This creates empathy, a sense of togetherness and a sharing of agendas and targets. Crucially, it increases efficiency and drives improved performance.

Many organizations, both public and commercial, are finding that the changes that are going on at a local, national and global level are providing new opportunities for rethinking how they do things. Organizations are increasingly working more collaboratively with other organizations.

For example, in education, schools are working more with other schools and with public services, voluntary and community organizations and the commercial sector to develop and provide extended services. The same is true for other public and private organizations. The following example is taken from the targeted youth support remodelling pathfinder.

Remodelling case study: Hampshire Local Authority – example of shared leadership

As Hampshire is a large county authority, the targeted youth support remodelling pathfinder focused on one area, the Test Valley, which includes a rural area and an area of deprivation.

The targeted youth support change team worked closely with the Turn Around project, a subgroup of the local strategic partnership, to ensure young people are participating in all decisions about community development. The change team is also liaising closely with Test Valley Foyer, an organization that provides a range of housing for young people, and operates in the pathfinder area to ensure the housing needs of young people are fully understood and addressed.

In addition, the change team is ensuring that housing will have a strong presence in the multi-agency targeted youth support team, as housing and neighbourhood renewal is recognized as a priority concern for young people and having them onboard will make the team more effective.

Young people are also now contributing to the development of neighbourhood activities. The targeted youth support remodelling process has provided an opportunity for young people to become more actively involved in the design of services and facilities intended for them. This is expected to result in many more appropriate and targeted activities for young people, which should lead to reductions in negative behaviours.

Communities

Organizational change usually involves a broad group of individuals and groups – that is, communities. It is therefore essential for those leading change to include all individuals and communities that will be affected by potential changes and, where appropriate, involve them in planning and delivery.

To achieve this, leaders need to work across four community domains:

- Building community *within* organizations. This is essential for supporting the demands of remodelling, continuing to raise standards and involving all staff in more active leadership roles.
- Building community *between* organizations. For the same reasons as above.
- Building community *between organizations and their local communities*. This involves, for example, local services and community groups and local businesses.
- Building *community in a multi-organization/multi-agency context*. This is probably the greatest challenge of all, as it touches on the values, beliefs, cultures and accepted norms of a wide cross-section of people, each of whom may feel they have the best option for change.

The development of the above communities means, of course, the end of the old *hero-leader* leadership model. This model was commonplace, for example, in schools, where headteachers sometimes saw themselves as endowed with superior knowledge and skills, almost single-handedly leading their school forward.

Similar examples of this type of leadership have also been commonplace in other organizations. In reality, of course, leadership is usually a little more complex than this. Nonetheless, in many public and private organizations it still remains vested in the hands of one person or a small number of individuals – and based around existing hierarchies.

The need now is to focus on *leadership* as much as on *leaders*; to promote new ideas of leadership and leadership behaviours, based around greater team-working and shared leadership authority.

The challenge that increased collaboration, personalization and the resulting shared leadership present will only be met if leaders and organizations actively *create* paths to the future.

The emerging and future context

Throughout this book the argument has been that our world is changing and that in the UK, and throughout most of the rest of the world, the industrial age is now over and we are moving into a new era marked by knowledge management, environmental concerns and a technological revolution. This requires a cultural shift as great, or greater, than that experienced in the eighteenth and early parts of the nineteenth century as the Industrial Revolution began to take hold.

Since 1997, the government's agenda has been underpinned by the recognition of a changing culture and the desire for equity matched with economic prosperity. For example, the publication of the Children's Plan (December 2007) moves the Every Child Matters agenda into its next phase and sets out an agenda for children, young people and their families until 2020.

In his book, *Leading in a Culture of Change* (2001), University of Toronto professor and worldwide authority on change Michael Fullan, describes the need for leadership that achieves and includes:

- a moral purpose – Fullan argues that leaders of any organization must have a moral purpose – this is critical to the organization's success;
- understanding change – we live in a change culture. It is no longer possible to 'do what we have always done' and presume that that will be acceptable. Leaders need to understand change and how people react to it if they, and more importantly the organizations, are to be successful;
- relationship building – Daniel Goleman (2004) and others have published widely on the importance of emotional intelligence. Relationship building is one key aspect of emotional intelligence and is found within the emotional management construct of emotional intelligence, as defined by Goleman;
- knowledge creation and sharing – the more understanding people have the more likely people will commit to the organization as long as the previous three constructs are in place. Fullan, however, expands on this logic and suggests that there are three issues that need to be well understood. People will not volunteer information unless they feel that they should for moral reasons. People will not willingly share information unless they believe that the dynamics of change make it imperative to do so. Finally, people will see information as merely a data glut unless there is a human relationship that turns it into information;
- coherence making – in order to make all this work, leaders need to build coherence. They need to ensure that everyone understands what is happening, why it is happening and how it fits with already existing agendas. This is a challenging and rewarding agenda because once people begin to understand how the system is working they are more likely to be willing to buy in.

Specifically, future leadership needs to: build trust, redesign jobs, change organizational structures and develop learning cultures.

Building trust

Traditionally, leadership roles have discouraged trust through placing accountability firmly in the hands of a designated leader. In the commercial sector this is reflected in the salaries, bonuses and resignation record of those at the top of the organization.

In the public sector, most leaders think that they are responsible for everything that goes wrong. This has been encouraged by the culture, expectations and training in the sector, even when this has encouraged distributed leadership. Building trust and taking risks can be a very courageous action in this context.

Redesigning jobs

In the future, jobs will be based on leadership *roles* rather than *tasks* that need doing. This implies the ability to release creativity from all staff members, recognizing their talents and skills and redesigning particular roles to suit individuals.

A good illustration of this shift is the growing importance of school business managers. As their role is non-teaching, these managers have the capability and capacity to oversee many of the new demands and agendas that schools face. For example, many of these managers are very involved in running and managing their schools' remodelling projects.

Changing organizational structures

To meet the demands of a fast and fundamentally changing world, organizations need to change at a structural level. A quick glance at the meteoric rise of the ultra-flexible web-based companies illustrates the vital importance of this. In particular, organizations need to develop a greater focus on teams and team collaboration.

Many of these teams will be multi-organizational or multi-agency. For leaders this requires recognizing that new leaders will emerge and that this needs incubation and nurturing – not always the easiest thing for established leaders to do. In effect, developing leaders of the future is a key role for the leaders of the present.

Developing learning cultures

As organizations collaborate more, there will be new and exciting opportunities to learn from each other, to develop greater understanding and deeper wisdom, and so improve performance.

Each of these developments requires a culture change. For leaders, there is a requirement to understand exactly what this culture change means for their organizations, customers and communities. In particular, it requires new models of leadership that recognize 'the importance of the connections between different issues, different individuals and different institutions' (NCSL, 2008b).

This is illustrated by the University of Warwick research into understanding the reasons why schools do or do not fully engage with the *Every Child Matters* and extended services agendas. The research team, led by Professor Alma Harris, reached a number of insightful conclusions (Harris et al., 2007), including two directly related to leadership:

1. Leadership is the key driver for change and the successful implementation of Every Child Matters and extended services (page 6). Effective leaders in this area need: negotiation skills; change management skills; brokerage ability; interpersonal skills; team building capability; ability to manage risk; financial acumen; and contextual literacy.
2. Schools that are fully implementing Every Child Matters and extended services are also fully engaged with workforce reform (page 6). There is a consistent and powerful interrelationship between workforce reform and effective Every Child Matters and extended services implementation. That is, remodelling provides change capability.

As a process, remodelling enables organizations to develop and deepen their understanding of the complexity of their current situation and become aware of key issues. It enables them to tap into all the intellectual, social and organizational capital in their own organization and, when working collaboratively, in other organizations. This enables them to develop and deliver appropriate and sustainable changes that improve their performance. This is most powerful when leaders work collaboratively in strong partnership with local communities.

Sustaining and leading change

A key challenge for the leadership of an organization is to ensure this is a *convergent* problem, not a *divergent* one. In simple terms, this means that organizations need to own the agendas through adapting national agendas to fit on their own terms and within their own individual context. At the same time, such agendas need to fit with the shared vision already operating within the organization and this may require an adaptation in order to accommodate it.

There is a danger that organizations can feel out of control and simply adopt the agendas they are being fed. This is a serious mistake. Agendas need to be understood and coherence in context needs to be realized. Remodelling is designed to deal with this scenario, but it has also been proven to work. As a result it is possible that the agenda can work for the organization and improve outcomes.

The requirements of successful leadership discussed earlier need to be underpinned by four key attributes, all of which can be learned and acquired (in fact the main challenge is often around leaders changing their mindset):

- The willingness to take risks and develop a no-blame culture. This is of primary importance. It requires the belief that others can take on leadership roles, and deliver and be accountable for results.
- The willingness to share leadership. There is a tendency for leaders to revert to command and control, particularly if they feel threatened or insecure. When this happens without a very

good reason, it limits future opportunities for delegation and shared leadership, destroys trust and fails to develop future leaders.

- The ability to inspire others and to listen. To develop creativity and innovation it is essential to inspire others to want to work with you and to develop their own leadership skills. This requires the ability to listen with empathy and so really hear how others feel and understand what they are passionate about.

- The skill to coach others to build a sustainable leadership culture. Succession planning is a key leadership role. Too often, organizations with strong leaders make great progress, but fall backwards as soon as the strong leaders move on. It is therefore vital that a structure is put in place to sustain and develop progress. This may well depend on building a coaching culture in which line managers are required to provide a more proactive and supportive environment – where those they lead begin to feel a more integral and valued part of the environment and better supported. For example, in schools the new performance management regime is supporting this for teachers and increasingly for all staff.

The NCSL notes that recent research within the NHS on leadership suggests:

> Leadership is the product of an organisation or unit's 'norms, routines and role definitions'. In other words, the function of the leader existed separately from the many different people who fulfilled the role depending on the circumstances. Klein also identified four key functions of the leader: providing strategic direction; monitoring team performance; instructing team members; and providing hands-on assistance when required.

> Klein's research suggests that organisations would do better to put in place the necessary structures to support whoever steps into a leadership position with well-established roles and clearly identified norms – than concentrate on selecting brilliant leaders. (NCSL, 2008, page 9)

Fundamentally, what is being suggested is that leadership is a system or a structure; that it is not a characteristic of particular individuals but rather of the organization as a whole. In this scenario, leadership is not held by a single person but is a shared role with clear accountability structures. An interesting part of this research discusses the need to put in place structures to support whoever is in these leadership roles. This is part what has become known in recent years as systems leadership.

In their book, *Understanding Systems Leadership* (2008), which particularly focuses on education, Collarbone and West-Burnham state:

> It is no longer a reality to continue to live in the educational world that served the industrial era so well. Those days have long gone. Nor is it possible for schools to continue

to exist in glorious isolation. The 'secret garden' began to vanish in the mid 1980s, the notion that the teacher was the sole person in charge has been under scrutiny since the late 1990s. Ideas around collaboration, partnership and multi-agency working are not in themselves new but the principles of trust and shared leadership in such relationships are. System leadership becomes a necessary phenomenon in such a context. (page 108)

The Innovation Unit, working with NCSL, develop this thinking when they suggest that in the foreseeable future the drivers for this type of leadership are likely to include:

- globalization – and the resulting requirement for universal proficiency;
- the media's pervasive impact on our deep culture;
- the internet, especially open source peer-to-peer systems/the ability to convene through the internet;
- an increasing emphasis on values. (Who are you? What do you stand for?);
- a huge rise in local affiliation/focus on the local community's needs;
- an increasing need for security;
- changing market opportunities and demands;
- exponential growth in user demands for personalized services;
- dissolving school (organizational) boundaries;
- new talents and skills.

(Innovation Unit, 2008)

These drivers, which were discussed in Chapter 1 of this book, identify the imperative for change and underpin the case for remodelling.

At the core of this emergent inclusive leadership is collaboration and partnership working, and demand-led public services embedded in personalization, and in extended services in local communities.

Developing effective leadership is a central tenet of remodelling and this provides a clear role for those who are leading organizations. To ensure successful remodelling, leaders need to support the change process, guiding change teams in seeking sustainable solutions.

At the same time, leaders need to maintain an overview of the way their whole organization operates, including all the internal processes and operations that make it work, and those outside that impact on the organization and other organizations in the partnership.

A core leadership role becomes providing coherence. For example, in public services, leadership roles such as the Director of Children's Services, the headteacher of a school, the director of a hospital trust or the CEO of a company are primarily facilitative.

This is expressed simply in the words of American business leader Warren Bennis: 'None of us is as smart as all of us. The Lone Ranger is dead' (cited in Craner, undated).

Developing leaders

Roland Barth, founding director of the Principals' Center at Harvard University, asks two key questions about leadership development:

- How are we training our leaders before they are appointed to lead others?
- Are they 'safe' before they begin to help others?

He uses the story of the oxygen mask on board an aircraft as an analogy. When airline staff run through their pre-flight safety routines, they always tell you to fix your *own* oxygen mask *before* you try to help your neighbour – i.e. unless you are safe yourself, you cannot help others.

As a country, England can be justifiably proud of the progress it has made over the last 10 years in understanding the nature and implications of leadership and in remodelling its leadership capabilities.

However, many organizations still have a tendency to revert to traditional industrial age thinking, particularly in periods of rapid change and disturbance or when they face a crisis. They revert to a command and control style of leadership, uni-directional procedures for carrying out tasks, hierarchical structures and a tendency towards cultures of blame.

Success in the twenty-first century

The good news is that there is another, much better, way. It is: to become the sort of organization that creates an inclusive and rewarding environment for all of its staff, with strong leaders who become even stronger – even more influential – by loosening their control and enabling and encouraging others to contribute more.

This type of organization recognizes the innate creativity and capability of each human being. It has systems in place that flatten its hierarchical structure and ensure its staff are deployed in appropriate roles with the necessary training, skills and commitment to provide an effective service to everyone.

This type of organization shares and develops its leadership. It recognizes that the risks it takes may lead to success or failure and it has a 'no blame' culture that encourages risks to be taken, nonetheless. Instead of writing off 'failures' and committing them to the dustbin, this type of organization learns from the experience and, as a result, changes and moves forward.

This type of organization operates in a way that addresses and capitalizes on the challenges of the twenty-first century. It is a learning organization; an organization that is flexible and alive to change. This type of organization is almost inevitably successful – not just in the short term, but into the long term.

The single most effective way for organizations to develop and succeed in this way is to work through the remodelling change process. And the choice to do this is, ultimately, the choice of leaders.

8 Sustaining change

The future is not a result of choices among alternative paths offered by the present, but a place that is created – created first in the mind and will, created next in activity.

The future is not some place we are going to, but one we are creating. The paths are not to be found, but made, and the activity of making them, changes both the maker and the destination.

(John Schaar, political theorist and Professor Emeritus at the University of California)

Change is inevitable and continual. It makes obvious sense for all of us to plan for it and actively manage and direct it in a way that leads to improvements in our lives. This is as true for businesses and other organizations, private and public sector, as it is for individuals.

It is imperative that organizations do their utmost to ensure the changes they make are for the best – whether it be improved and environmentally sustainable profit margins or improved and socially sustainable outcomes for children and young people.

This is of crucial importance to the success of organizations themselves. Even more significantly, it is of crucial importance for all our lives, for the lives of our children, and ultimately even for the health of our planet itself.

Planning and embedding change

Remodelling is not about change in itself. It is about how organizations and individuals approach change; it is about creating a fluid and flexible underlying organizational structure that enables and encourages continous change and progress – without disruption and with the full support and input of an empowered and highly motivated workforce.

This stops organizations rushing, as they very often do, into implementing knee-jerk solutions before they fully understand the root causes of the challenges they are facing.

It ensures that the solutions they develop address the real underlying issues – not simply immediate symptoms – and so results in long-term, highly-effective and sustainable change.

Remodelling is not, and never will be, a finished product. Rather, it is a dynamic and ever-developing cycle of continuous improvement that can be easily and powerfully adapted and tailored to address any individual organization and situation – large or small, simple or complex.

This inherent adaptability ensures that remodelling remains relevant, accessible, powerful and sustainable. It helps organizations direct and manage change and adapt, develop and succeed into the long term.

It is important to consider what long term means. Remodelling is intrinsically sustainable as it embeds a remodelling culture where all staff in an organization (or in a group of organizations) are collaboratively involved in leading and shaping change on an ongoing basis.

The process ensures the structural and operational focus of organizations is set firmly on successful change and improvement (internal and external), not just for the duration of the initial change process, but also into the medium- and long-term future in a fluid and continous remodelling cycle of improvement.

For many organizations this involves a fundamental change of mindset. Most organizations, for example, aspire to be, or applaud themselves on being, open to new ideas, to being innovative and creative – and many of them are.

The problem, though, lies in these organizations' underlying structure and culture. As this is often inflexible, a great many organizations tend to zig-zag their way forward, lurching from side to side in clumsy response to each new technology and each new idea. Like an addiction, each movement results in a high and often in improved performance in the short term, but it also comes with a low – yet another demotivating and demoralizing change for the workforce. In the end this leads to unhappy and burnt-out workers and diminishing returns.

Remodelling is not a new piece of kit or yet another new and 'revolutionary' idea to be used in the short term and then thrown away when another comes along. Rather it is a living and developing process, a method, that embeds a remodelling culture in organizations where the skills, ideas and knowledge of *all* of their workforce – managers, backroom and front-line staff – are sought, appreciated, harnessed and applied in a positive and highly effective way in an ongoing basis.

This enables organizations to successfully negotiate the experience – the inevitable ups and downs – of change. It helps workers and organizations deal effectively with the rational, practical nuts and bolts, aspects of change, and with its often more intangible political and emotional facets.

As described in Chapter 2, the remodelling change management process grew out of the commerical sector. Through practical usage it has been honed and adapted to work successfully in all environments, organizations and change situations.

Developed predominantly by Consulting Strategies Limited for use in the public sector (and deployed by the National Remodelling Team and, latterly, the Training and Development Agency for Schools), the process has been tried, tested and proven – and continues to be tried, tested and developed.

It has been used on a national scale to successfully help a range of public organizations address a variety of very different and complex challenges and changes. These include the introduction of the requirements of the National Agreement, extended services in and around schools, targeted youth support, and a range of associated projects.

There have been many complex challenges (for example, introducing new roles, new working practices, changes in focus, overcoming resitance and intrangisense, and so on), but by bringing together all staff and stakeholders to address and develop changes, these challenges have all been overcome – one by one.

Without the structured method that remodelling provides, it is highly unlikely these major changes would have been introduced so successfully.

Challenges

As the world becomes more and more connected, and the global village of the early 1970s more of a reality, the complexity of change environments is increasing. What was once quite obviously and definably local, now generally needs to be seen in a larger context.

The Cabinet Office's strategy unit published a consultation document in February 2008 that predicts:

- By 2020 China will be the second, and India the sixth, largest economy in the world.
- The global population is expected to rise from 6.5 billion people in 2005 to 7.7 billion in 2020 and 9.1 billion in 2050.
- There will be increasing effects of climate change and increased pressure on global resources. (page 20)

The document argues that Britain is very capable of meeting the many challenges that are already arising, particularly the changing global context. However, it also points out that Britain needs to prepare for these challenges and be ready to turn them into opportunities. Key to this is ensuring that the population has the necessary knowledge, skills and attributes to deal with this scale of change. This explains why the education and training participation age is rising to 18 years of age by 2015, and why considerable funding and resources are focused on adult education.

Increasingly, organizations are having to work with different languages and within different international cultures. In addition, the internet and other new communications and delivery channels mean that local organizations are being forced, willingly or unwillingly, to compete at a national, often global, level.

The targets and accountabilities of organizations and workers are becoming more complex as a result and, more and more frequently, organizations are working collaboratively (internally and externally) to benefit from the extra expertise, delivery capability and economies of scale this provides.

This creates an even greater need for sophisticated skills, in-depth knowledge and understanding, and appropriate training. It also means that organizations need to develop systems and processes that allow them to work collaboratively on an equal basis, with shared leadership and aims.

This includes developing processes that enable them to improve and develop into the long term; to help them to create a shared vision for the future, and shared plans that ensure they realize this vision.

Remodelling gives organizations the method and flexibility they need to do this. To change, improve and succeed on an ongoing basis within both straightforward and complex environments. It helps them address the limitations of their old top-down 'do it alone' management models and fully capitalize on the ideas and skills of all their workforce.

It releases capacity, energy and creativity and builds connections between all of the workforce – and between organizations – that enables organizations to progress. It helps them build a common vocabulary and common targets, share data, work more creatively together, improve efficiency, and capitalize on different perspectives and wider expertise.

Ultimately, remodelling helps individual organizations to focus more on individuals – both inside and outside the organizations themselves. It helps them deliver a more and more personal service to a customer base that is increasingly demanding – increasingly expecting – a fully personalized, altogether more 'human', service. And in today's knowledge age this is the secret of true and lasting success.

References

Argyris, C. (1999) *On Organizational Learning (2nd Edition)*, Oxford: Blackwell Publishers

Axner, M. (2007) *Promoting Coordination, Cooperative Agreements, and Collaborative Agreements Among Agencies*, Lawrence: The Community Tool Boxm, http://ctb.ku.edu

Barth, R.S. (1991) *Improving Schools from Within: teachers, parents, and principals can make the difference*, San Francisco, CA: Jossey-Bass Education Series

Beckhard, R. and Harris, R.T. (1987) *Organizational Transitions: Managing Complex Change (2nd Edition)*, Indiana: *Addison Wesley*

Bentley, T. and Wilsdon, J. (2003) *The Adaptive State: strategies for personalizing the public realm*, London: DEMOS

Blanden, J. and Machin, S. (2007) *Recent Changes in Intergenerational Mobility in Britain*, London: The Sutton Trust

Blandford, S. (2005) *Remodelling Schools Manual: workforce reform*, Harlow: Pearson Education

Bubb, S. and Earley, P. (2004) *Managing Teacher Workload: work–life balance and wellbeing*, London: Paul Chapman Educational Publishing

Collarbone, P. (2003) Launch speech of the NRT

Collarbone, P. and West-Burnham, J. (2008) *Understanding Systems Leadership*, London: Network Continuum Education

Collins, J. (2001) *From Good to Great*

Conner, D.R. (1993) *Managing at the Speed of Change: how resilient managers succeed and prosper while others fail*, New York: Random House

Craner, S. (undated) Interview with Warren Bennis, www.managementskills.co.uk/articles/ap98-bennis.htm

DCLG (2006) *Strong and Prosperous Communities: the Local Government White Paper (Volume 1)*, Norwich: HMSO

DCSF (2007a) *The Children's Plan: building brighter futures*, London: Stationery Office

DCSF (2007b) *The Early Years Foundation Stage Guidance*, Nottingham: DCSF Publications

DCSF (2008) *Building Brighter Futures: next steps for the children's workforce*, Nottingham: DCSF Publications

DfES (2003) *Excellence and Enjoyment: a strategy for primary schools*, Nottingham: DfES Publications

DfES (2004) *Every Child Matters: Change for Children*, Nottingham: DfES Publications

DfES (2005) *Youth Matters Green Paper*, Nottingham: DfES Publications

DfES (2007) *Care Matters: Time for Change*, London: Stationery Office

Easton, C., Eames, A., Wilson, R., Walker, M. and Sharp, C. (2006) *Evaluation of the National Remodelling Team (NRT): year 3*, Slough: NFER Research Publications Every Child Matters – Targeted Youth Support ttp://www.everychildmatters.gov.uk/deliveringservices/targetedyouth support/

Feinstein, L. (2003) 'Inequality in early cognitive development of British Children in the 1970 cohort', *Economica*, 40: 73–79

Financial Management in Schools (2008) www.ncsl.org.uk/managing_your_school/financial_management/index.cfm

Fullan, M. (2001) *Leading in a Culture of Change*, San Francisco, Cal: Jossey-Bass

Fullan, M. (2003) *Change Forces with a Vengeance*, London; RoutledgeFalmer

Gardner, H. and Laskin, M. (1996) *Leading Minds*, New York: Basic Books Publishers

Goleman, D. (2004) *Emotional Intelligence & Working with Emotional Intelligence (Omnibus Edition)*, London: Bloomsbury Publishing

Goleman, D. (2007) *Social Intelligence: the new science of social relationships*, London: Arrow Books

Hamel, G. (2002) *Leading the Revolution: how to thrive in turbulent times by making innovation a way of life (2nd Edition)*, Boston, Mass: Harvard Business Press

Harris, A., Allen, T. and Goodall, J. (2007) *Understanding the Reasons why Schools Do or Do Not Fully Engage with the ECM/ES Agenda*. TDA and NCSL, available online at: www.tda.gov.uk/upload/resources/pdf/e/ecm_report_september_final_0907.pdf

HM Government (2002) *Education Act 2002*, Norwich: Stationery Office

HM Government (2004) *The Children Act 2004*, Norwich: Stationery Office

HM Government (2006) *The Education and Inspections Act 2006*,. Norwich: Stationery Office

HM Treasury (2003) *Every Child Matters*, London: Stationery Office

Himmelman, A.T. (1995) *Communities Working Collaboratively for a Change*, Minneapolis, Min: The Himmelman Consulting Group

IBM Global Business Services (2007) *Unlocking the DNA of the Adaptable Workforce: the global human capital study 2008*, Somers: IBM Global Services

Innovation Unit (2008)Next Practice, system leadership, www.innovation-unit.co.uk/education-experience/next-practice/system-leadership

Kolb, D.A. (1984) *Experiential Learning: Experience as the Source of Learning and Development*, London: Financial Times/Prentice Hall

Kotter, J.P. (1996) *Leading Change*, Boston, Mass: Harvard Business School Press

Kotter J.P. and Cohen, D.S. (2002) *The Heart of Change: real life stories of how people change their organizations*, Boston, Mass: Harvard Business School Press

Kubler-Ross, E. (1997) *On Death and Dying*, Columbia: Scribner Classics

Leadbeater, C. (2004) *Personalisation Through Participation: a new script for public services*, London: DEMOS

Learning and Skills Council (2006) *The London Learning and Skills Plan: our regional commissioning plan for London 2007–2008*, London: Learning and Skills Council

Leitch, S. (2006) *Prosperity for All in the Global Economy – world class skills*, Norwich: Stationery Office

NCSL (2008a) *The Future of Leadership*, Nottingham: NCSL Publications

NCSL (2008b) www.nscl.org.uk/publications/publications-systemleadership.cfm

NRT (2003) *Touching Tomorrow*, London: National Remodelling Team, www.tda.gov.uk/upload/resources/pdf/t/touchingtomorrow.pdf

NRT (2005) *Transforming the School Workforce: what is remodelling?*, London: National Remodelling Team

Ofsted (2007) *Reforming and Developing the School Workforce*, London: Ofsted Publications

Papert, S. and Caperton, G. (1999) *Vision for Education: the Caperton–Papert Platform*. Essay written for the National Governors' Association meeting held in St Louis, Missouri

PricewaterhouseCoopers (2001) *Teacher Workload Study*. London: PricewaterhouseCoopers (for the DfES)

PricewaterhouseCoopers (2007) *Independent Study into School Leadership*, Nottingham: DfES Publications

Radclyffe School, Oldham (2008) website www.theradclyffeschool.co.uk/

RSA Opening Minds website, http://www.thersa.org.uk/newcurriculum/index.asp

Schein, E.H. (2004) *Organisational Culture and Leadership (3rd Edition)*, San Francisco, Calif: Jossey-Bass

Scholtes, P.R. (1998) *The Leader's Handbook: making things happen, getting things done*, New York: McGraw-Hill

Senge, P. (1996) 'Introduction' in *Synchronicity: the inner path of leadership*, edited by Jaworski, J., San Francisco: Berrett-Koehler Publishers

Senge, P. (2006) *The Fifth Discipline: the art & practice of the learning organization (2nd Edition)*, London: Random House Business Books

Social Partnership, 2003. *Raising standards and tackling workload: a national agreement*, London: DfES

Strategy Unit (2008a) *Realising Britain's Potential: future strategic challenges for Britain*, London: The Cabinet Office

Sutton Trust (2007) News Release, December.

TDA (2005a) National Agreement Case Studies www.tda.gov.uk/remodelling/nationalagreement/resources/casestudies.aspx

TDA (2005b) *2005–2008 Corporate Plan*, London: TDA Publications

TDA (2007) School Improvement Planning Framework, DVD

TDA (2008) *The Little Book of Managing Change*, London: TDA Publications

TDA (2008b) Extended Schools Case Studies www.tda.gov.uk/remodelling/extendedschools/resources/casestudies.aspx

TDA publications website www.tda.gov.uk/about/publicationslisting/list.aspx

TDA (2006) Remodelling www.tda.gov.uk/remodelling.aspx

Turner, S. (2002) *Tools for Success: a managers guide*, Maidenhead: McGraw-Hill Professional

Walton, M. (1992) *The Deming Management Method*, New York: Mercury Business Books

Weisbord, M. and Janoff, S. (1995) *Future Search: action guide for finding common ground in organizations and communities*, San Francisco, Calif: Berrett-Koehler

Wheatley, M.J. (2007) *Finding Our Way: leadership for an uncertain time*, San Francisco, Calif: Berrett-Koehler Publishers

Index

adaptability of remodelling 106
adaptable workforce 5, 6
adaptive states, and leadership 93
adult education 107
age, education and training participation
     age 107
agencies, and school change teams 82

Banbury School, Oxfordshire 77–9
Barth, Roland 102
Bennis, Warren 101
Bentley, Tom 93
brainstorming, and school change teams 78
Brigshaw High School and Language
     College 82–8
*Building Brighter Futures: Next Steps for the
     Children's Workforce* (DCSF) 11
bullying 37–8
bursars, and school change teams 81
business tools, and the remodelling
     process 43, 44

Cabinet Office strategy unit 107
Care Matters: Time for Change 11
Carey, Julia 71
catering arrangements in schools, and change
     teams 82–4, 87–8
change curve
  and change teams 75
  and the remodelling process 6, 14, 45–6, 52

change teams xii, 17, 69–89
  and facilitative leadership 61
  inclusive 60, 64–5, 70–2
  leading 74
  numbers of 73
  proactive and inclusive 60, 64–5
  in the public sector 75
  rational, political and emotional aspects
     of 66, 75
  and the remodelling process 48, 54
  schools
    attributes of 76
    Banbury School 77–9
    Brigshaw High School and Language
      College 82–8
    membership of 78–82
    remodelling stages 77
  setting up 72–4
  and shared leadership 95
childcare, and extended services 29
The Children's Plan 3, 10, 11, 97
Clark, Stuart 85–6
Cleaver, Kevin 72
coherence building, and leadership 97
collaboration 108
  in change teams 71
  constructive 59, 63
  and leadership 95, 96
Collins, Jim, *From Good to Great* 4
communities, and leadership 96, 99

complexity of organizational change 66–7
consortium schools, Leiston consortium 33–8
constructive collaboration 59, 63
Consulting Strategies Limited (CSL) 15, 107
continuous improvement, remodelling cycle of 55–6, 106
core elements of remodelling 59–67
creativity, and leadership 91, 92, 100
CSL (Consulting Strategies Limited) 15, 107
cultural change
    and leadership 97
    in schools 16–17
culture, inclusive 59, 62–3

deepen stage
    of the remodelling process 47, 51–2, 56
    and change teams 77
deliver stage
    of the remodelling process 54–5, 56
    and change teams 77
Deming, W. Edwards 13
Department for Children, Schools and Families (DCSF) 11
    Youth Support Team 40–1
develop stage
    of the remodelling process 53–4, 56
    and change teams 77
Dinning, Alan 49
discover stage
    of the remodelling process 47, 49–51, 56
    and change teams 77
Duran, Joseph M. 13

Early Years Foundation Programme 11
Education Action Zone (Excellence in Cities) 33, 36
Einstein, Albert 60
Ellowes Hall Secondary School, Dudley 23
Elms, Mark 24
embedding change 105–7

emotional change curve 6, 14, 45–6, 52, 75
emotional considerations
    and change teams 75
    making remodelling work 60, 65–6
emotional intelligence 97
employment
    changing model of 3, 4, 9
    leadership roles and job redesign 98
European Union 7
evaluation workshops 54
Every Child Matters: Change for Children 10
Every Child Matters agenda xii, 10
    and extended services in and around schools 28, 29
    and leadership 97, 98–9
    and the Leiston consortium 34
    and school improvement planning 31, 32
    and targeted youth support 38, 39
Excellence in Cities, Education Action Zone 33, 36
exclusions, and school change teams 89
experiential learning 14
extended schools coordinators, and school change teams 80–1
extended schools programme 28–30, 33, 107
    and leadership 70, 98–9

facilitation
    facilitative leadership 60–1
    leading change teams 74
    and the remodelling process 44
financial management 25–6
flexible organizations 4
FMiS (Financial Management in Schools) 25–6
Fowle, Mark 20
Fullan, Michael 61
    Leading in a Culture of Change 97

Gateshead Local Authority 30–1
generic deepening workshops 52

Gibson, Joan 61
global context of change 2–3, 108
globalization
   and leadership 101
   and remodelling 14
Goleman, Daniel 97
governors, and school change teams 82
guiding coalition, and change teams 69

Hammond, Janette 78
Hampshire Local Authority, example
   of shared leadership 95–6
Harris, Alma 98–9
Hayer, Hardial 20
headteachers, and school change teams 79–80,
   82, 88–9
Hippey, Lynn 86–7
HLTA (higher level teaching assistant)
   standards 22
homework clubs in schools 29
Horton Lodge School, Staffordshire 18

inclusive change teams 60, 64–5, 70–2
inclusive culture 59, 62–3
Independent Study into School Leadership
   (PricewaterhouseCoopers) 31, 69–70
Innovation Unit, on leadership 101
intellectual capital 4, 92
internet, and leadership 101

Jones, Nick 76
journey-mapping workshops 52

knowledge creation and sharing, and
   leadership 97
Knowsley Local Authority, targeted youth
   support 40
Kotter, John 61, 69
   Leading Change 46

Lao Tzu 27
Laurence, Peter 82, 88–9

Leadbeater, Charles 94
leadership xii–xiii, 14, 91–103
   building trust 97–8
   changing nature of 4
   and collaboration 95
   and communities 96, 99
   development 102
   effective 5, 6
   emerging and future context of 96–9
   energizing practice 93–4
   and job redesign 98
   and learning cultures 98–9
   and organizational structures 98
   and partnership working 93, 95
   and personalization 93, 94–5, 96
   redefining the role of 92
   remodelling and leadership in
      schools 69–70
   and the remodelling process 51
   shared and effective 59, 60–1, 92, 99–100
      case study (Hampshire Local
      Authority) 95–6
   sustaining and leading change 99–101
   teams in schools 31
   in the twenty-first century 102–3
   and workforce modernization 93, 94, 99
Leading Change (Kotter) 46
Leading in a Culture of Change (Fullan) 97
learning cultures, and leadership 61, 98
learning organizations 102–3
legislation, Children and Young People's Bill
   (2008) 11
Leicester City, targeted youth
   support in 39, 40
Leiston consortium 33–8
Leitch Report 3, 7–8
Lenners, Simon 83–4
local change 3
London Leadership Centre Consortium 15,
   16, 21
long-term planning, and the remodelling
   process 56

looked-after children 11
Lydbury North Church of England School,
    Shropshire 19

Maclean, Deborah 79
managers, and the remodelling process 48–9
Mitchell, Sandra 65
mobilize stage
    of the remodelling process 47–9, 56
        and change teams 77
moral purpose, and leadership 97
multi-agency working xi
    and extended services in and around
        schools 28
    and leadership 96
    and the remodelling process 47, 51

National Agreement xi, 10, 21–2, 24–5, 27, 107
    and change teams 82
    and extended services in and around
        schools 28
    implementation 32–3
National Foundation for Educational Research
    (NFER), evaluation reports 15, 30
National Remodelling Team 107
NEETs (not in education, employment and
    training) 89
NHS (National Health Service)
    leadership 100
Nicholls, Mary 73
no-blame cultures, and leadership 99, 102
NRT (National Remodelling Team) 21, 22–5
    extended services in and around
        schools 28–30
    and financial management 25–6
    and Leiston consortium 35
    and the TDA 27–8

options development workshops 54
organizations
    challenges facing 3–5
    changing 6–7, 98

imperative for change 1–2
organizational culture and change
    teams 64, 70–2

parenting support 29
parents, and school change teams 81, 89
partnerships
    benefits of 30–1
    and leadership 93, 95
    and the remodelling change process
        56–7
passive approach to change 1–2
Patanjali 13
Penryn College, Cornwall 25
personalization, and leadership 93, 94–5,
    96
planning change 105–7
political considerations
    and change teams 75
    making remodelling work 60, 65–6
premises managers, and school change
    teams 81
PricewaterhouseCoopers, study of leadership
    in schools 31, 69–70
private sector leadership 93, 95
proactive change teams 60, 64–5
professionalism, and the remodelling change
    process 56
project managers, and the mobilize stage of
    the remodelling process 48
Prosperity for All in the Global Economy
    (Leitch Report) 3, 7–8
proven change process 60, 65
public sector
    change 7–9
    change teams 75
    leadership 94–5, 95, 98
pupils
    pupil conferences 35
    and school change teams 81–2, 84–5,
        86, 88
Purcell, Janet 85

Radclyffe School, Oldham 20
Raising Standards and Tackling Workload:
    a national agreement (Social
    Partnership) xi, 10, 21–2
rational considerations
    and change teams 75
    making remodelling work 60, 65–6
Reforming and Developing the School
    Workforce (Ofsted) xi, 15
relationship building, and leadership 97
remodelling process 43–57
    business tools 43, 44
    complexity of 67
    emotional change curve 6, 14, 45–6, 52
    facilitation 44
    five stages 46–57
        deepen 47, 51–2, 56, 77
        deliver 54–5, 56, 77
        develop 53–4, 56, 77
        discover 47, 49–51, 56, 77
        mobilize 47–9, 56, 77
    sustaining 55–7
    and targeted youth support 43, 47, 48–9,
        50–1, 55, 57
risk and resilience workshops 52

Schaar, John 105
school business managers
    and leadership 98
    and school change teams 81
school improvement planning 31–2, 37
    and leadership 70
School Workforce Pathfinder (TSWP) 15–16,
    18–20
security and leadership 101
Senge, Peter 1, 61, 92
senior leaders, and school change teams 80
senior management, and the remodelling
    process 53
services, and school change teams 82
Simpson, Debbie 86–7
social equity, and public sector change 8–9

special interest clubs in schools 29
sponsors, and the mobilize stage of the
    remodelling process 48–9
staff
    and constructive collaboration 63
    and facilitative leadership 60–1
    and inclusive culture 62–3
    and leadership 91
    and the proven change process 65
    and school change teams 80–1,
        85–8
stakeholders
    and change teams 74, 76
    and constructive collaboration 63
    and facilitative leadership 60–1
    and inclusive culture 62–3
    and leadership 91
    and the proven change process 65
    and the remodelling process 48, 49, 50, 51,
        53, 59
Strong and Prosperous Communities
    (Local Government White Paper) 9
succession planning, and leadership 100
support staff, and school change teams
    80–1
sustaining change 105–8
sustaining the remodelling process 55–7
Sutton Trust 8
Swales, Chris 87–8
systems thinking 14

talent management 5, 6
targeted youth support 38–41, 107
    change teams 72–3
    and the remodelling process 43, 47, 48–9,
        50–1, 55, 57
    and shared leadership 95–6
TDA (Training and Development Agency for
    Schools) 22, 27–8, 107
    and change teams 77, 81
    and Leiston consortium 36
    remodelling process 43–57

TDA (Training and Development Agency for Schools) (*Cont'd*)
  and school improvement planning 31–2, 37
  and targeted youth support 40–1
teachers
  Leiston consortium 34, 36
  and the National Agreement 21–2
  and school change teams 80
  shortages 16
  and the TDA 27–8
  workload 15–16, 18
teaching assistants, and school change teams 80
Teaching and Learning Responsibility payments 36
technological revolution 2
  and leadership 97
tensions, and the remodelling process 56
Tidemill Primary School, Lewisham 24
total quality management (TQM) 13–14
trust, leadership and building trust 97–8
TSWP (School Workforce Pathfinder) 15–16, 18–20
Turner, Suzanne, *Tools for Success* 44

Understanding Systems Leadership (Collarbone and West-Burnham) 100–1
Unlocking the DNA of the adaptable workforce (IBM survey) 5

values, and leadership 101
Vaughan, Paul 40

WAMG (Workforce Agreement Monitoring Group) 21
Wheatley, Margaret, *Finding Our Way: Leadership for an Uncertain Time* 4
Wilsdon, James 93
work/life balance, and school change teams 80
workforce
  development 4–6
  modernization and leadership 93, 94, 99
  remodelling 106
Workforce Agreement Monitoring Group (WAMG) 21
workforce reform, and the TDA 28

Youth Matters Green Paper 38, 39
youth support *see* targeted youth support